box cars and one-eyed jacks™

On A Roll To Spelling...
And More

Written by:

Joanne Currah
Jane Felling

"Box Cars" won the National Learning Disabilities Association Idea of the Year 1991.

© 1995 BOX CARS & ONE-EYED JACKS™
ISBN: 0-9695276-6-7

DEDICATION

Dedicated To The Currah Crew

 is for Richelle, my right hand girl… really remarkable!

 is for Connor, my little commander and a cool character too.

 is for Mackenzie, my middle marvel full of magic.

 is for Madison, my miniature masterpiece on the move.

 is for Cameron who continues to control all chaos as our "charming chief" in charge.

You're the Best!

Love, Joanne.

For my number one team;

Chris, Andrea and John who,

without a doubt, make it all worthwhile.

Love, Jane

TABLE OF CONTENTS

GAME	LEVEL	SKILLS	PAGE

Introducing the Alphabet and Its' Sounds

Spelling Simple to Complex Words

Spelling Fun with All Kinds of Words

Puzzlers, Brainstormers and Word Games

Sentence Construction and Parts of Speech

Reproducibles 109
General Bibliography 138
About the Authors 140

Introduction

The publication of <u>On a Roll to Spelling and More</u> marks a new beginning for us. We are thrilled to be taking our Box Cars success in mathematics and launching the format in an equally important curriculum area <u>Spelling and Language</u>.

Like many of our ideas the games have been around for awhile in draft form. I remember clearly a plane ride where Joanne showed me a game she had developed for spelling. Her daughter Richelle had helped her create the rules and strategies - and to say the least it was a great game that Richelle played eagerly. (See Let'ter Roll, p. 70)

At the time Joanne had used one of our favourite die - the 30-sided die, to generate letters. Our original idea was to create just the one game, put it in a box with a score pad and be done. That was two years ago! With the development of our spelling and language games came the long search and development of the special alphabet dice that are included. We are proud of what we've created.

The timing has never been better to publish a book of spelling and language games. Listening to teachers and parents around the country as we travel and give workshops we have been constantly asked for ideas to help children with spelling. Again the challenge was to go back to our classroom roots to find strategies, tips and ideas we implemented in our programs to help children with spelling and language. You will see this reflected in both the chapter headings and games.

In a sense we've come full circle. Years ago our consulting started in the language area. We gave hundreds of workshops on early reading and writing strategies and we would do these little "Box Cars Breaks" to break up the day with a little math fun! We are both looking forward to facilitating new language workshops that will bring fun & enjoyment to students and teachers in this curriculum area.

People ask what's next?... Well, we're working on it!

Joanne and Jane

Why Games to Teach
Spelling and Language?

Games are highly motivating and filled with opportunities to develop many concepts and skills. First and foremost, games generate language and require players to engage in purposeful problem solving and thinking. Our title <u>On a Roll to Spelling and More</u> was carefully chosen. The "More" firstly refers to going beyond spelling activities and including many other language concepts games. "More" importantly it is essential to our philosophy that the games provide opportunities for learners to think about a concept as they play. Learners must employ and test out their thinking and strategies and learn from their playing experience. As learners repeatedly engage in challenging games they learn from their mistakes, form generalizations and broaden their understanding of the concept. A good teaching strategy must take into account the various needs of students, the modes of sensory input (visual, auditory, kinesthetic - tactile) and the cognitive processes, involved in learning to spell and use language. Games incorporate all of a student's senses. They see, hear and touch when they play.

Spelling and language learning can be fun and still remain purposeful. We believe it is the special quality of "playfulness" that makes games an invaluable resource to teachers, parents and students.

Before we began the development of the games for this book we reflected on the ways we taught spelling and language concepts in our classrooms. As we brainstormed the strategies we realized that many of them could form the basis of a game. The rules were written in such a way that a learner can repeatedly practise a concept, skill, rule, mnemonic trick, etc. Within the context of the games experience learners will need to spell, speak, identify and use language effectively.

We also reflected on how language is learned and practised. Language develops through predictable, sequential stages of development. It can only develop with practise by making successive approximations. In a supportive environment language and spelling become closer to standard, acceptable form. In our games learners are constantly talking, showing, experimenting and making decisions, verbalizing strategy, and modeling for one another. The opportunity to test out, experiment, make mistakes and learn from that experience enables learners to progress in their development. Most importantly the games context allows the development to happen with support.

HOW TO USE THIS BOOK

<u>On a Roll to Spelling and More</u> contains 64 games and is divided into the following 5 sections. A detailed description of the types of games included in each follows at the end of this section.

1. It's As Easy as ABC! Introducing the Alphabet and Its' Sounds
2. Spelling Simple to Complex Words
3. Spelling Fun with All Kinds of Words
4. Puzzlers, Brainstormers and Word Games
5. Sentence Construction and Parts of Speech

The games are organized into sections that reflect the common strategies for teaching spelling and other language concepts. Within each section the games are organized using the following format:

PLAYERS:	number needed for playing - intended to be flexible. competitive, cooperative or solitaire.
LEVEL:	appropriate grade level, intended to be flexible.
SKILLS:	specific language or spelling skills are listed.
EQUIPMENT:	specific items are listed.
GETTING STARTED:	rules and instructions which can be changed to meet individual or group needs.
VARIATIONS:	ideas to increase or decrease difficulty or to change/ add a skill.
TEACHING TIPS:	Some games have Teaching Tips and are identified by this symbol in the margin. ☐ Tips will provide specific suggestions for teaching a rule, strategy or concept within the context of that game.
JOKES:	Enjoy our attempt at humor! Maybe the jokes can be placed on the board in the morning for the students to solve and the answers shared at the end of the day. Everybody needs a good laugh!

The games do not have to be played in a set order, however each section has been arranged in order of difficulty. Teachers and parents can select games to:

1. introduce a concept or skill
2. practise a concept or skill
3. master a concept or skill

Section I - It's As Easy as ABC!
Introducing the Alphabet and Its' Sounds

The simplest games are found in this section and are a logical starting point for teaching beginning spellers. Spelling must incorporate an understanding of the alphabet - the 26 letter names, the more than 40 sounds they make and the common combinations / patterns of letters that comprise the words of our language. This section contains alphabet recognition and initial sound games and are perfect for developing pre-reading and writing skills. In this section we've provided opportunities for children to learn the basic phonetic principles and establish correct sound/symbol relationships. Many words they will first attempt to spell are phonetically correct ie., rhyming families. Our spelling system is not totally random. If we establish basic alphabetical principles spelling can get off to a good start. As early as possible we want children to know which letter combinations are probable/possible and which are not ie., qu probable; kw not probable.

Section II - Spelling Simple to Complex Words

This extensive section includes games to focus on word beginnings and word endings, vowels, common letter combinations, word middles, syllabication and the use of dictionaries. Throughout this section watch for TEACHING TIPS for rules and strategies that can be taught with the games.

Section III - Spelling Fun with All Kinds of Words

Included in this section are games that allow students to explore rhyming concepts, graphic cues, compounds, antonyms, synonyms, jail and silent letter words. Children have a natural curiousity about unusual types of words. These games will allow students an opportunity to explore them!

Section IV - Puzzlers, Brainstormers and Word Games

This section contains games that may take longer periods of time to complete. They are challenging games that develop vocabulary, spelling fluency, decision making and logical reasoning. To be successful children will have to incorporate their understanding of common/probable letter combinations. Children will become successful after many opportunities to play and test out their strategies.

Section V - Sentence Construction and Parts of Speech

All of the games in this section are intended for older students. Games to practise building simple to complex sentences and vocabulary are included. The parts of speech games include explorations of nouns, verbs, adjectives, adverbs and propositions.

Materials

The strength of <u>On a Roll to Spelling and More</u> is the simplicity of the materials. All that is required to play the games are the following:

1. Alphabet Dice - for classroom use we recommend 1 die per pair or group of students.

These special alphabet dice are hard to resist and may go missing, so for consistency we count out and collect the dice before and after each games period.

The dice need to be rolled on a flat, level surface. Children will quickly learn to "telescope" down and read the number on top of the dice.

2. Regular Spotted Dice - 1 pair per child

3. Paper / Pencil or Mini Chalkboards / Chalk

4. Reproducible Gameboards - if they are needed it will be specified in the **Equipment** section of the rules.

5. Alphabet tiles - players can use these to build words as they play.

Alphabet Tiles

To take into account the various needs of students, and the modes of sensory input; visual, auditory and kinesthetic, we recommend that alphabet tiles/letters be used during play. Students can roll their letters with the die, take the corresponding letter tiles (a good matching activity in itself), and build words, puzzles, gameboards as they play. The alphabet tiles provide a visual as well as tactile manipulative experience while the learner is practising spelling and language. The tiles provide an alternate to paper and pencil practice. The tiles may be moved about easily without the frustration of erasing! Scrabble letters, magnetic letters, etc. can be used or see the order form for resources.

6. Games journal for students to record and save their games, reflect and write about strategies used, concepts practised, etc.

7. Dictionaries and thesaurus.

Classroom Organization

THE GAMES CLASSROOM IS AN ACTIVE CLASSROOM! The games classroom is a dynamic, interactive place. Students will learn a great deal from talking with one another. Sharing and reflection throughout the games period is an important part of the learning process. When students play there will be lots of talk. Be a good "language detective" and circulate as students are playing. By listening to their talk teachers often hear evidence of a student's growing understanding of a concept or discover an opportunity to intervene with questions that further develop student understanding.

Organizational Formats

Games can and should be a regular classroom teaching strategy. All students can benefit from consistent playing and practise time. Teachers should implement a schedule that fits both their classroom and timetable needs.

The following organizational suggestions have been shared with us over the years and may provide insight into various classroom implementation formats.

1. A short 10 - 15 minute playing time is scheduled each day. The first day of the week the game is taught to the whole group. The group practises over the week to develop and strengthen the concept, skills or strategy of the game. This is often coupled with No. 2.

2. A longer 30 - 50 minute game block is scheduled once a week. The game is learned and practised for a sustained playing time. Follow up play periods are offered during center time or free time.

3. Try cross graded practise with a "buddy classroom". Many teachers pair two different leveled classes ie., Grade 2 and 4, 3 and 6, etc. for a 30 - 50 minute game block once a week. The benefits include peer teaching and modeling, improved self-esteem and continued development of language and spelling concepts.

4. Spelling Game Back Packs: Copyright permission is given to teachers to copy the games and send them home with students for practise. See page 135 for our ideas published in the B.C. Prime Areas article "Math Game Back Packs".

Teaching the Games

The games are usually taught to the entire group first using the overhead projector or by demonstration on the floor. It is best to have the group play the game for several play periods so that is is well understood. After a number of games have been taught students or teachers can choose a game that would be most appropriate for them to play. Eventually, during a typical games period, many different games will be played.

One other teaching strategy that works very well is to teach one small group a specific game. This group practises and becomes the "Experts" for this game. Over the course of the week they each take another small group or pair and teach them the game. By the end of the week the whole class is playing! More importantly the benefits to learning and self-esteem are tremendous. This quote by William Glasser sums up the effectiveness of this teaching strategy.

WE LEARN

10%	of what we read
20%	of what we hear
30%	of what we see
50%	of what we both see and hear
70%	of what is discussed with others
80%	of what we experience personally
95%	of what we teach someone else

William Glasser

Some Final Thoughts

On a Roll to Spelling and More should complement your existing language program, not replace it. It is in this spirit that we hope On a Roll to Spelling and More will be helpful to both teachers and parents and the children they teach.

Finally, HAVE FUN!

–Joanne and Jane

It's as easy as...

Introducing the Alphabet
and Its' Sounds

DISAPPEARING ALPHABET

PLAYERS: Solitaire or 2

LEVEL: Pre-Kindergarten and up

SKILLS: Letter recognition

EQUIPMENT: One thirty-sided alphabet die, gameboard (see reproducibles), pencil

GETTING STARTED: The goal of the game is to be the first player to cross off all the letters in the alphabet. Player one rolls a B and crosses B off their gameboard. Players alternate turns until one player has no letters left on their gameboard. If a player rolls a ☆ the player may choose any letter to cross off.

VARIATION: To increase the difficulty have players verbalize the sound of the letter and/or a word that begins or ends with the letter ie., S - the player crosses this off and verbalizes "<u>s</u>andwich" or "dre<u>ss</u>".

 TEACHING TIP:

Have children print the letter in the air or trace this letter onto their palm, or partner's back.

Show me a girl who's allergic to the alphabet...

And I'll show you B-hives!

FROM A TO ZEE

PLAYERS: Solitaire or 2

LEVEL: Pre-Kindergarten and up

SKILLS: Printing upper and lower case letters

EQUIPMENT: One thirty-sided alphabet die, gameboard (see reproducibles), pencil

GETTING STARTED: The goal of the game is to build the alphabet from A to Z. Each player needs their own gameboard. Choose either the lower or upper case variation. Player one rolls the die and records this letter in the appropriate space. If a player rolls a ☆, that player may choose any letter to print on their gameboard. If a player rolls a letter previously rolled the next player proceeds. The first player to correctly fill in their alphabet gameboard is the winner.

VARIATION: After the die is rolled the player may connect the upper and lower case letters. Fifteen connections and you win.

 TEACHING TIP:

After the child records their letter have them close their eyes and visualize that letter in their favourite colour.

TEACHER: What bug can you find in the alphabet?

ANDREA: B!

18

ABC BINGO

PLAYERS:	2 - 4
LEVEL:	Grade 1 and up
SKILLS:	Letter recognition
EQUIPMENT:	One thirty-sided alphabet die, 1 blank 20-squared gameboard (see reproducibles), coloured bingo chips or other markers, paper and pencil
GETTING STARTED:	Players take turns rolling the die, verbalizing the letter rolled and filling this letter into any blank square of their choice on their gameboard. When all twenty squares have been filled players are now ready to begin play.

Player one rolls the die and verbalizes the letter rolled. If the letter rolled is a letter that was previously recorded on their board that player covers this square(s) with their marker(s). Players take turns rolling the die and covering squares. If a letter rolled is not on the board the next player rolls. If a ☆ is rolled, a player may choose any letter. The winner is the first player to cover four letters in a row horizontally, vertically or diagonally. Players can king a space on their board by re-rolling an identical letter.

VARIATION I: The winner must also verbalize outloud the sound of each letter.

VARIATION II: Before covering squares with their marker(s), players must verbalize a word that begins or ends with this letter.

TEACHING TIP:

This game could be played on mini-chalkboards. Have students create a grid with twenty spaces and fill in with letters, as per rules.

TEACHER: A, B, C, D, E, F, G –
What comes after G?

RICHELLE: Whiz!

BINGO BLASTERS

PLAYERS:	2
LEVEL:	Kindergarten - Grade 1
SKILLS:	Letter recognition, sound / symbol
EQUIPMENT:	One thirty-sided alphabet die, one gameboard per player (see reproducibles), bingo chips
GETTING STARTED:	Each player has their own thirty-squared letter Bingo Blaster card. Player one begins by rolling their alphabet die and verbalizing the name of the letter. They may cover this letter with a bingo chip. If a ☆ is rolled, player one may cover any square of their choice.
	Player two now rolls a letter, identifies the letter rolled and covers it with a bingo chip on their own gameboard. Players continue to alternate turns. If a letter rolled is already covered, that player misses a turn and their opponent proceeds. The winner is the first player to cover five squares in a row horizontally, vertically, or diagonally.
VARIATION:	The player must also spell a word beginning or ending with the letter rolled before this letter can be covered.

TEACHER: What has 5 eyes but cannot see?

CHRIS: Mississippi River!

HOW DOES IT SOUND?

PLAYERS: 2

LEVEL: Pre-Kindergarten - Grade 1

SKILLS: Associating the letters of the alphabet with the correct sounds, printing

EQUIPMENT: One thirty-sided alphabet die, gameboard (see reproducibles), paper and pencil

GETTING STARTED: The goal of the game is to be the first player to correctly make the sound of at least fifteen letters on the alphabet die. Players alternate rolling the die and making the appropriate sound of the letter rolled ie., if a B is rolled, the player makes the "b" sound. If a player is correct this letter is recorded by that player. If the player is not correct, no letter is recorded. Players alternate rolling the die until one player has recorded at least fifteen different letters. If a player rolls a letter they have already correctly sounded out and recorded, they may roll again. If a player rolls a ☆ they may choose any new letter to sound out.

 TEACHING TIP:

There are only twenty-six letters in the alphabet, but more than forty sounds in spoken English. In this game start with the basic sounds of each letter (use short vowel sounds to begin).

TEACHER: Richelle, please spell "banana".

RICHELLE: B-a-n-a-n-a-n-a ... I know how to spell it, but I don't know when to stop!!

22

STAND UP!

PLAYERS: Small groups or whole class

LEVEL: Kindergarten and up

SKILLS: Letter recognition, letter printing, initial consonants, vowel sounds

EQUIPMENT: One thirty-sided alphabet die, paper and pencil

GETTING STARTED: Each player secretly records five different letters on paper. One player is selected to be the designated roller for their group. This player rolls and calls out the letter and its' corresponding sound. When a letter called out appears on a player's list, that player crosses this letter off their list. Players continue listening for letters and crossing off any letters rolled until one player crosses off all five letters. This player then stands up and is the winner of that round. If a ✶ is rolled, the die is re-rolled.

VARIATION I: When the player stands up that player must also verbalize five words that begin or end with their five letters. ie., s, h , m, r, and o

"snakes, horses, mice, rabbits, owls"

VARIATION II: To increase the difficulty players may also earn 1 point for each correctly spelled word.

VARIATION III: To practise sentence construction players must stand up, verbalize words beginning with their five letters and use all five words to create a meaningful sentence.

ie., "Snakes, horses, mice, rabbits, and owls can all be found in the zoo."

Show me King Kong playing cards with the Jolly Green Giant and I'll show you a big deal!

ALPHABETICAL ROLL

PLAYERS:	2
LEVEL:	Grade 1 and up
SKILLS:	Letter sequencing, alphabetizing
EQUIPMENT:	One thirty-sided alphabet die
GETTING STARTED:	Player one rolls the die and calls the letter rolled out loud. The player also verbalizes in sequence the next three letters that follow that letter in the alphabet ie., player rolls an F and verbalizes "F..G..H..I". If the player is correct, one point is earned. If a player rolls a ☆, the player may choose any letter and name the three letters that follow (exceptions are Y and Z). The first player to earn ten points is the winner.
VARIATION I:	The players roll the alphabet die and must name the three letters that precede the letter rolled ie., M is rolled and player verbalizes "J..K..L".
VARIATION II:	After the player names the next three letters in alphabetical sequence they must verbalize a word that begins with each letter ie., N is rolled, player verbalizes "O..P..Q and the words Open, Popcorn, Quietly".
VARIATION III:	Players extend **variation II** by challenging each other to alphabetize and create words that fit into a specific category. Players refer to the Categories Reproducible on page 125.
	ie., player one rolls a "C" for Countries or Cities and verbalizes "Nigeria, Ottawa, Pakistan, Quebec"

Q: What four letters of the alphabet do you use to play hide and seek?

A: O I C U

RHYMING SNAPPERS

PLAYERS:	2
LEVEL:	Grade 1 and up
SKILLS:	Identifying rhyming pairs
EQUIPMENT:	One thirty-sided alphabet die
GETTING STARTED:	Player one rolls the die and both players identify the starting letter. Both players try to be the first player to give a rhyming pair. One of the words must start with the letter rolled. If a ☆ is rolled, the die is re-rolled.
EXAMPLE:	Player one rolls a B
	Player two verbalizes "Bag/Rag" and earns 1 point. Players may earn additional points by spelling their words, or by identifying the "rhyming chunk" "ag"
	Players alternate rolling the die. After a set period of time the player with the most points is the winner.
VARIATION:	To increase the level of difficulty the players must name three or four rhyming words and/or spell them outloud.
	ie., Roll = N
	"Nice, rice, twice, and slice", or "New, drew, stew and flew" would all be acceptable answers.

 TEACHING TIP:

There are many word families that share the same sound-symbol pattern. "Rhyming families" are great to work on to establish early success in spelling.

Spelling Simple to Complex Words

From...

cat

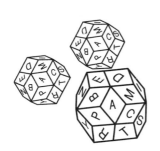

TO

CATASTROPHE

WORD RACE

PLAYERS: Solitaire or 2

LEVEL: Kindergarten and up

SKILLS: Creating 3 letter words, ending sounds, middle sounds

EQUIPMENT: One thirty-sided alphabet die, one sound gameboard per player (see reproducibles), pencil

GETTING STARTED: Players alternate rolling the die and filling in letters on their gameboard. Players fill in the spaces that are open and try to create correctly spelled words. Players are allowed a total of 5 reject rolls throughout the course of the rolls. If a ☆ is rolled players may select a letter of their choice. If a vowel is rolled a player may re-roll. Players keep rolling until one player has filled in all of the spaces in one or all rows of their gameboard.

EXAMPLE: See reproducibles for other Word Race Gameboards.

ra___	su___	pa___
ru___	sa___	pu___
re___	se___	pe___
ri____	si___	pi____
ro___	so___	po___

The player who has created the most correctly spelled words is the winner.

VARIATION: Players may allow four or five letter words to be created for points ie.,

rice

rink

ripe

rich

To create words with more than three letters the players must roll one letter at a time.

VOWEL CROSSES

PLAYERS:	2
LEVEL:	Grade 1 and up
SKILLS:	Spelling simple 3 letter words
EQUIPMENT:	One thirty-sided alphabet die, one gameboard per player (see reproducibles)
GETTING STARTED:	The goal of the game is for players to fill in their gameboard with as many correctly spelled words as possible. Players alternate rolling the die and calling the letters outloud. If a player rolls a ☆ they may choose a letter of their choice.
	A total of thirty rolls will be taken during the game. Throughout the rolling players may place the letters into any space on their gameboard. Any roll may be rejected by either player and placed into the reject spaces. Once a letter is placed into any space it cannot be changed or erased. After thirty rolls are completed players count up the number of correctly spelled three-letter words. The player with the most correctly spelled words is the winner.
VARIATION:	To increase the difficulty players may alter the gameboard to include various double vowel combinations (see reproducibles).
EXAMPLE:	

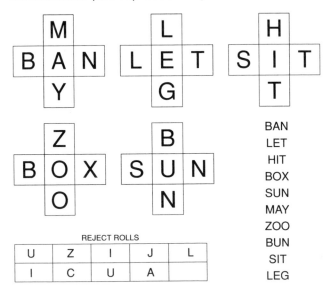

SCORE: 10/10 - 1 reject left

UP TO YOUR NECK IN WORDS

PLAYERS: 2 or more

LEVEL: Grade 1 and up

SKILLS: Spelling simple words

EQUIPMENT: One thirty-sided alphabet die, one gameboard per player (see reproducibles), pencil

GETTING STARTED: Player number one rolls the die, identifies the letter and spells a simple word starting with this letter. The player prints this word in the appropriate space on their gameboard. Players alternate turns rolling the die and filling in their gameboard. The spaces do not need to be filled in sequentially.

If a ☆ is rolled the player chooses any letter to record. The first player to fill in all spaces with correctly spelled words on their gameboard is the winner.

VARIATION: For older students words can be scored 1 point per letter ie., ball = 4 points   cabbage = 7 points, etc. Calculators may be used to figure out final scores.

EXAMPLE:

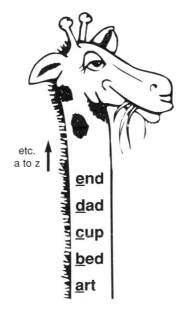

etc.
a to z

end

dad

cup

bed

art

WHAT'S IN A NAME?

PLAYERS: 2 - 4

LEVEL: Grade 1 and up

SKILLS: Word recognition, spelling familiar first and last names

EQUIPMENT: One thirty-sided alphabet die, paper and pencil

GETTING STARTED: The goal of the game is to be the first player to correctly spell three different names. Classmates, family members, first or last names (even pets) may be included.

Players alternate rolling the die, recording only the letters they have rolled. Players continue rolling and building their own letter banks until one player has correctly spelled three different names.

If a player rolls a letter already rolled the player may choose to record this letter a second time or roll again for a new letter. Some names have more than one of the same letter.

If a player rolls a ☆ they may record any letter of their choice.

EXAMPLE: Letters Rolled Include:

b, s, f, n, a, j, d, o, p, t, and h

Acceptable Answers Include:

Jan, Dan, Joan, John, Pat, Dot

 TEACHING TIP:

Teach the concept that all names begin with a capital letter.

Q: Who drinks up all the water in the bathtub?

A: Dwayne

BEG-ENDERS

PLAYERS: 2

LEVEL: Grade 2 and up

SKILLS: Spelling simple words

EQUIPMENT: One thirty-sided alphabet die, paper and pencil

GETTING STARTED: The goal of the game is to be the first player to correctly spell a word that begins and ends with the established letters. To begin, the die is rolled to establish the starting letter and a second time to establish the ending letter ie., M is the starting letter and T is the ending letter. Players now alternate rolling the die and recording each letter. The player rolling has the first chance at spelling a word that fits the established criteria. If a player cannot make and spell a word on their roll, they pass and let their opponent have a try. If neither player can spell a word the next player rolls the die and records another letter. If a ☆ is rolled the player may select any letter of their choice.

EXAMPLE: Roll : M - start and T - end

Player 1 rolls D pass   Player 2 pass

Player 2 rolls W pass   Player 1 pass

Player 1 rolls J   pass   Player 2 pass

Player 2 rolls A and spells MAT and scores 3 points (1 point per letter).

Players alternate starting each new round. The player with the most points after a set number of rounds is the winner.

VARIATION I: To decrease the difficulty players roll beginning and ending letters and verbalize any word beginning and ending with these letters to earn a point. Double points are earned for correctly spelling the word.

VARIATION II: To increase the difficulty, players refer to the "categories reproducible" p. 125 and roll the alphabet die to select the category for that round. Players then proceed to play "Beg-Enders" with the challenge of creating a word that also fits into the selected category.

RACE TO SPELL

PLAYERS: 2 or teams of 2 vs. 2

LEVEL: Grade 2 and up

SKILLS: Spelling two, three, and four letter words

EQUIPMENT: One thirty-sided alphabet die, paper and pencil

GETTING STARTED: Each player needs their own paper and pencil to record the letters rolled. The goal of the game is to be the first player to make a two letter word, three letter word, four letter word and so on. (Plurals do not count).

Player one rolls the die and all players record this letter on their paper. Players alternate rolling the die and recording the letters. Repeat letters are also recorded. If a ☆ is rolled the roller may select a letter of their choice.

When any player notices a combination of letters that spell a two letter word they say "Spell It" and spell their word. If they are correct, they score 2 points (one point per letter). Play continues with the next roll. Players now try to find a three letter word (worth 3 points) and so on.

Play continues until a four and five letter word have been created. Players total their points for the round. A new roller is selected for the second round. Play continues for a set period of time. The player with the most points is the winner.

CHRIS: Mom could you help me with my spelling homework?

MOM: No Chris, it wouldn't be right.

CHRIS: That's okay Mom, as long as you give it a try.

ALPHABET ROLL OUT

PLAYERS: Teams of 2 vs. 2

LEVEL: Grade 2 and up

SKILLS: Spelling simple words

EQUIPMENT: One thirty-sided alphabet die, gameboard (see reproducibles), pencil, dictionaries are optional

GETTING STARTED: STEP ONE: Dividing the alphabet letters between both teams. At the end of step one each team will have 13 different letters of the alphabet assigned to them. These letters will be used in the spelling portion of the game.

Each team alternately rolls the die and records the letter rolled on to their spelling sheet. As well, after each roll this letter is crossed off the master alphabet choot and cannot be used again. If that letter is rolled again it cannot be used and the team must re-roll to get a new letter. If a ☆ is rolled the team may select any letter of their choice that is left on the master alphabet sheet. Step One is completed when both teams have selected their half of the twenty-six alphabet letters.

EXAMPLE: Team one's rolls included:

M Z (rolled M again, re-roll) I Q G T R H
N (☆ - selects) O P C and V

Team two's rolls included:

K J F W Y E L (rolls Y again, re-roll) B (rolls I again, re-roll) (☆ - selects) S A (☆ - selects) U D and F

When both teams have thirteen letters the spelling portion of the game begins.

STEP TWO: Teams now have ten minutes to create as many two, three, four and five letter words, etc.

SCORING:
two letter words = 2 points
three letter words = 3 points
four letter words = 4 points, etc.

At the end of the set spelling time players exchange lists to check for spelling accuracy. Dictionaries may be used to double check for accuracy.

Final scores are determined. The team with the most points is the winner.

35

MEMORY WORDS

PLAYERS: 3

LEVEL: Grade 2 and up

SKILLS: Spelling simple words

EQUIPMENT: One thirty-sided alphabet die, paper and pencil

GETTING STARTED: One player is selected to be the recorder for the round, the other two players will be the rollers. These two players alternate rolling and naming the letters rolled. The recorder prints the letters out of view of the other two players as they are rolled. The other two players must remember the letters rolled. Players attempt to say a word that is spelled with some or all of the letters that have been previously rolled. When a ☆ is rolled, the die is re-rolled.

After a player calls out a word that contains some or all of the rolled letters, the recorder checks for accuracy. The player must spell the word correctly and the recorder verifies that the letters have in fact been rolled. If the player is correct, 1 point is earned, and a new round of play begins.

EXAMPLE: Letters rolled in sequence are as follows:
c y r l a d

The following would be acceptable words:
card yard lard car lay day lad ray

If both players call out the same or different words at the same time and both words are accepted by the recorder, then both players earn 1 point. Play continues until one player earns 5 points. This player then becomes the recorder for the next round.

VARIATION: Before play begins, players may determine the minimum number of letters per word ie., only four letter words or more are accepted.

card yard lard

 TEACHING TIP:

Children need many opportunities to practise auditory memory as in the above game. In this game we have players chant back through the letters rolled, silently ie., "inside their heads" after each new roll.

A MITT FULL OF VOWELS

PLAYERS:	2
LEVEL:	Grade 2 and up
SKILLS:	Identifying vowels, spelling simple words
EQUIPMENT:	One thirty-sided alphabet die, one regular die, paper and pencil
GETTING STARTED:	The goal of the game is to correctly spell a word containing the vowel indicated on the regular die and the starting letter indicated on the alphabet die. Players use the following legend for the regular die.

Roll 1 = A
Roll 2 = E
Roll 3 = I   } Teachers may wish
Roll 4 = O   to take a blank cube
Roll 5 = U   and mark with letters
Roll 6 = Y or Roll Again

Player one begins by rolling both dice and identifying the starting letter on the alphabet die and the vowel to be used. If a ☆ is rolled, player may select any letter of their choice.

EXAMPLE:	Roll = P and 3
	Player one spells PITCH. Player one scores 1 point per letter. In this example player one would earn 5 points. Player two now takes their turn. Players continue to alternate turns. The first player to score 100 points is the winner.
VARIATION:	Concentrate on Long or Short vowels only.

 TEACHING TIP:

TEACH THE RULE: All words have at least one vowel!

In any of the simple spelling games have children trace and draw a shape around their word. Have them visualize this shape when spelling the word a second time ie.,

pitch   p i t c h

VOWEL DOUBLE DUTCH

PLAYERS: 2

LEVEL: Grade 2 and up

SKILLS: Spelling simple words containing double vowels

EQUIPMENT: One thirty-sided alphabet die, two regular dice, paper and pencil

GETTING STARTED: The goal of the game is to be the first player to correctly spell a word with the corresponding starting letter and vowels. Play begins by rolling both regular dice. The alphabet die determines the starting letter for the word and the regular dice determines which vowels must be used. Players should use their discretion should an improbable double vowel combination occur ie., uu. Players use the following legend to determine the vowel:

Roll 1 = A
Roll 2 = E
Roll 3 = I   } Teachers may wish
Roll 4 = O   to take a blank cube
Roll 5 = U   and mark with letters.
Roll 6 = Roll Again

EXAMPLE: Player one: Rolls S and 4/5 = OU

Players must think of and spell an "ou" word starting with the letter S. Some possible answers include: "soup, source, and sound".

Player two: Rolls B and 1/2 = EA

Players must think of and spell an "ea" word starting with the letter B. Some possible answers include: "beast, beat, bean and beard".

The first player to correctly spell an appropriate word scores a point. The dice are re-rolled for the next round. If a ☆ is rolled the roller may select any letter of their choice. Play continues for a set period of time. The player with the most points is the winner. At the end of the game words can be collected and categorized by vowel combinations.

TEACHER: Where did the astronaut put his peanut butter sandwich?

CONNOR: In his <u>launch</u> box.

38

DICTIONARY DAZE

PLAYERS:	2 to 4
LEVEL:	Grade 3 and up
SKILLS:	Spelling - word building, using a dictionary
EQUIPMENT:	One thirty-sided alphabet die, dictionary, paper and pencil
GETTING STARTED:	The goal of the game is to be the first player to roll the appropriate letters to spell a minimum of five words on one specific dictionary page. The player must also read the definition of these words outloud to the other players in order to earn 1 point for each correctly spelled word.
	Players alternate rolling the die and recording all the letters rolled by all the players. If a player rolls a ☆ the player may select any letter of their choice. The first player to record five correctly spelled words on their dictionary page wins.
EXAMPLE:	Letters Rolled Include:
	N R F H S A D E M R Y T
	Player one records and defines:
	Far, Farm, Farmer, Fast, Faster

TEACHING TIP:

Guide words can help students locate their words. They are found at the top of each page, usually they are in heavier or bolder type. The left hand guideword is the first entry word to appear on the page and the one on the right is the last. Telephone books work the same way!

SPEAKING OF DICTIONARIES...

Q: Where can you ALWAYS find money?

A: In the dictionary.

IT'S ALL IN A WORD

PLAYERS: Teams of 2 vs. 2

LEVEL: Grade 3 and up

SKILLS: Spelling simple to complex words

EQUIPMENT: One thirty-sided alphabet die, two regular dice, paper and pencil

GETTING STARTED: The goal of the game is to be the first team to correctly spell a word that contains the letter indicated by the roll of the die.

One player rolls the dice and both teams identify the letter. If a ☆ is rolled players may select any letter of their choice. This letter must be used in the spelled word. Teams next identify how many times this letter must appear in the word. Teams may choose to either add or subtract the dice to determine the quantity. Doubles are automatically a re-roll, except for double 1's.

EXAMPLE: Roll = D   and 5/3

Team two spells SADDLE (they chose to subtract 5 - 3 = 2 and used two D's in their word).

The first team to print an acceptable word scores 1 point. The first team to earn 10 points is the winning team.

TEACHING TIP:

Pronunciation is very important to spelling. Have children slow down and pronunciate each syllable carefully ie., <u>Wed</u> <u>nes</u> <u>day</u> making sure to represent each sound. Every syllable needs a vowel.

TEACHER: What is the capital of Canada?

MADISON: The letter C.

POSITIONS PLEASE

PLAYERS:	Teams of 2 vs. 2
LEVEL:	Grade 3 and up
SKILLS:	Spelling complex words, letter position
EQUIPMENT:	One thirty-sided alphabet die, one regular die, timer, paper and pencil
GETTING STARTED:	The goal of the game is to correctly spell words with the rolled letter in the correct position. Team one rolls both dice. The regular die indicates the ordinal position that the letter indicated on the alphabet die must be positioned. If a ☆ is rolled, the die is re-rolled. Both teams have from one to three minutes to spell a suitable word.
EXAMPLE:	Roll = W and 5. Teams must now spell a word that matches the roll ie., a word with a W in the fifth position. This word may begin with any letter. Team one spells "screws" and team two spells "thrown".
	SCORING: Teams score 1 point per letter for their correctly spelled word. In the above example both teams would earn 6 points.
	Team two now rolls the dice for the next round. Play continues until one team earns 75 points.
VARIATION:	Teams may spell as many words as possible in the given time period. Score 1 point per letter and play to 200 points.
	ie., Team one creates and spells correctly:
	screws
	software
	sidewalk
	Team one earns 22 points.

 TEACHING TIP:

Having students construct their own mnemonic tricks will help them learn difficult or tricky spellings, especially homonyms.

Examples: a p<u>ie</u>ce of p<u>ie</u>   a fr<u>ie</u>nd to the <u>end</u>   <u>too</u> contains t<u>oo</u> many <u>o's</u>
          a <u>sea</u>l in the <u>sea</u>   the princi<u>pal</u> is your <u>pal</u>

FIT IN THREE

PLAYERS:	2 or teams of 2 vs. 2
LEVEL:	Grade 4 and up
SKILLS:	Spelling three letter words and larger
EQUIPMENT:	One thirty-sided alphabet die, paper and pencil
GETTING STARTED:	The goal of the game is to correctly spell words containing the three letters rolled by your opponent. Player one rolls the die three times. Each letter is recorded by player number two. Player two must correctly spell words (any length) containing the three letters within the established time limit (three - five minutes). Correctly spelled words earn a player 1 point per letter.
EXAMPLE:	Roll: = T, A, and L. Team two spells TALENT and scores 6 points, ALERT and scores 5 points for a total of 11 points. Other acceptable answers may include later, tall, lantern, etc.
	After the allotted time is over the players reverse rolls. Player two now rolls the die and player one spells as many words as possible that include all three letters rolled.
	If a ☆ is rolled the spelling player may select any letter of their choice. Play continues for a set period of time. The player with the most points is the winner.
VARIATION I:	COMPETITIVE PLAY - The die is rolled three times and letters are recorded. The first player to correctly spell a word containing the three letters scores 1 point per letter. The dice are then re-rolled for round two.
VARIATION II:	The die is rolled three times and letters are recorded. Both teams or players create as many words as possible during the allotted time. The player or team with the most correctly spelled words earns 1 point.

 TEACHING TIP:

To speed up play, team two can establish their letter and length of word to be spelled at the same time as team one. Both teams may work on their words at the same time.

SUCCESSFUL SYLLABLES

PLAYERS: 2

LEVEL: Grade 4 and up

SKILLS: Spelling multi-syllable words

EQUIPMENT: One thirty-sided alphabet die, one regular die, paper and pencil

GETTING STARTED: Players roll both dice and refer to the following legend for the game.

ROLL 1 - 2   spell a one syllable word

ROLL 3 - 4   spell a two syllable word

ROLL 5 - 6   spell a three or more syllable word

The goal of the game is to correctly spell a word with the correct number of syllables starting with the letter indicated on the alphabet die. Player one rolls the dice and determines the starting letter and the number of syllables for their word. If a ☆ is rolled, the die is re-rolled. Player has a set time limit (one to three minutes) to correctly spell and/or record their word. If the player is correct then they score 1 point per syllable. Players continue to alternate turns. After a set number of rounds the player with the most points is the winner.

EXAMPLE: Roll = 3 and M. The player must spell a two syllable word starting with the letter M.

"Money, marry, movie" would all be acceptable responses and the player would earn 2 points.

VARIATION I: Allow players to verbalize as many correct answers as possible during the allotted time and the players earn one point for each correct response.

VARIATION II: Play a speed variation with three players. One player is the roller and the other two players race to be the first player to respond correctly to earn a point.

 ***TEACHING TIP:***

Teach the concept: Every syllable has a vowel. In a two syllable word ending in e, it's usually a y.

SYLLABLE SNAP BRAINSTORMERS

PLAYERS: 3 or teams of 2 vs. 2

LEVEL: Grade 4 and up

SKILLS: Spelling multi-syllable words

EQUIPMENT: One thirty-sided alphabet die, one regular die, paper and pencil

GETTING STARTED: The goal of the game is to be the first player to correctly spell a word with the appropriate number of syllables starting with the letter indicated on the alphabet die. Players alternate rolling both dice and refer to the following legend for the game:

ROLL 1-2   Spell a two syllable word

ROLL 3-4   Spell a two/three syllable word

ROLL 5-6   Spell a three/four syllable word

The dice are rolled and players determine the starting letter and number of syllables needed for their word. If a ☆ is rolled, the die is re-rolled. The first player to spell an appropriate word scores a point. If players give their answer at the same time, then both players score a point.

EXAMPLE: Roll = P and 5

Player one spells <u>pa</u> <u>ra</u> <u>chute</u> and scores 1 point.

The first player to score 20 points is the winner.

VARIATION: Play a non-competitive variation. Allow players to spell as many words as possible during the allotted time. The player or team with the most correctly spelled words earns 1 point.

DICE TOSS CHALLENGERS

PLAYERS: Teams of 2 vs. 2

LEVEL: Grade 4 and up

SKILLS: Spelling up to twelve letter words

EQUIPMENT: One thirty-sided alphabet die, two regular dice, paper and pencil

GETTING STARTED: The goal of the game is to correctly spell words beginning with the letter rolled in a certain time limit. Team one begins by rolling the alphabet die to determine the first letter for spelling. Team two rolls the 2 regular dice to determine the length of the word team one must spell. ie., Rolls M on the alphabet die and 4+3 on the regular dice: 4+3 = 7. Team one must correctly spell a seven letter word beginning with the letter M within the established time limit (three to five minutes). Correctly spelled words earn team one 1 point per letter ie., team one would earn 7 points for correctly spelling "magpies".

Teams now reverse roles and team two now has their turn spelling. If a ☆ is rolled the spelling team can select the starting letter.

Some roll combinations may be next to impossible ie., a two letter word starting with Q or X. Teams should use their discretion and re-roll when appropriate.

Play continues for a set period of time. The team with the most points is the winner.

VARIATION: COMPETITIVE PLAY - Both the alphabet die and regular dice are rolled at the same time. Both teams now race to be the first team to correctly spell a word of the correct length and starting letter.

 *TEACHING TIP:*

To speed up play, team two can establish their letter and length of word to be spelled at the same time as team one. Both teams may work on their words at the same time.

WORD GIANTS

PLAYERS: 2 - 4 or teams of 2 vs. 2

LEVEL: Grade 4 and up

SKILLS: Spelling complex words

EQUIPMENT: One thirty-sided alphabet die, paper and pencil

GETTING STARTED: The goal of the game is to be the first player to create a minimum ten letter word from which that player must find at least two "mini-words", within that word. Players alternate rolling the die and calling the letters outloud. If a player rolls a ☆ they may choose a letter of their choice. Players should record the letters as they are rolled. Once a player is able to spell at minimum a ten letter word they verbalize outloud "Word Giant". That player must now verbalize and spell at least two "mini-words" within their giant word. Players earn 3 points for the "giant word" and 1 point for each "mini-word". The first player to score 30 points is the winner.

EXAMPLE: Letters rolled include:

E X S A T M F N T E O D R

The giant word created was:

DEMONSTRATE

"The "mini-words created were

1. demon		5. rate
2. on		6. at
3. demo		7. ate
4. rat		

The player would earn 10 points for the round.

 TEACHING TIP:

For spelling large words, the strategy of breaking down the word into smaller bits (as in the above example) can help. Also have the child pronounce the word differently ie., together = "to" "get" "her".

DICTIONARY SNAP

PLAYERS: 3

LEVEL: Grade 4 and up

SKILLS: Using a dictionary

EQUIPMENT: One thirty-sided alphabet die, two dictionaries

GETTING STARTED: The goal of the game is to be the first player to locate the given word in a dictionary. One player is designated as the "roller/word caller", the other two players are the "searchers". The roller rolls the die and calls out any word starting with that letter ie., Roll = P and the player verbalizes PEN. The searchers now have to find PEN in the dictionary. The first player to do so scores a point.

VARIATION: The goal of the game is to be the first player to locate a given name in a telephone book. Items could also be called out beginning with the selected letter, and the searcher would locate this item in the "yellow pages" of the telephone book.

 TEACHING TIP:

Players may wish to rotate "jobs" ie., the "roller" and "searcher" with each roll.

To find a word in a dictionary a player needs to understand alphabetical sequencing. Play Alphabetical Roll p. 24 with at least a few letters (starting letter helps) of the word. A knowledge of common letter combinations also helps ie., qu not kw. Also see Dictionary Daze p. 39 for other tips.

TEACHER: How do you spell weather?

ANDREA: W-E-O-T-H-E-R

TEACHER: That's the worst spell of weather we've had in a long time.

47

DICTIONARY DOOZERS

PLAYERS: 2 or teams of 2 vs. 2

LEVEL: Grade 3 and up

SKILLS: Spelling complex words

EQUIPMENT: One thirty-sided alphabet die, one regular die, one dictionary per player, paper and pencil

GETTING STARTED: The goal of the game is for each player to stump an opponent with their "doozer" word and to spell their own doozer word given to them by their opponent.

To begin each player rolls the alphabet die to determine the starting letter of the doozer word they will give to their opponent. Each player needs their own dictionary to assist them in selecting the doozer word of their choice.

For example, if player one rolls an I, that player may choose "Insurance" as their doozer word to present to their opponent. Prior to choosing their doozer words players may want to limit the maximum number of letters allowed ie., a twelve letter word, etc. Players may also limit the length of time allotted for their doozer word search ie., three minutes maximum.

The player also rolls the regular die to determine how many incorrect letters and/or incorrect positions of letters they will be allowed when attempting to spell their "doozer words".

For example, if a two is rolled, players are allowed two errors within the word they are spelling and may ask their opponent for two clues ie., Examples of clues may be

"Does it have an e at the end of the word?"
"Is there a silent b?"
"Are there two d's in this word?"

Players are still entitled to earn 1 point for the word if it is spelled correctly after their two clues. If a player spells their opponent's doozer word perfectly with no assistance an automatic 5 points is earned. Each player is allowed one minute to spell their word.

DICTIONARY DEADLINE

PLAYERS: Solitaire, 2, or teams of 2 vs. 2

LEVEL: Grade 3 and up

SKILLS: Creating words with a minimum of 2 letters, using a dictionary

EQUIPMENT: One thirty-sided alphabet die, dictionary, paper and pencil

GETTING STARTED: The goal of the game is to create as many words as possible using a dictionary and letters which have been placed into a "letter bank". To begin each player builds their letter bank by rolling their die fifteen times and recording each roll. If the same letter is rolled it is recorded a second or third time. If a ☆ is rolled, that player may choose any letter to record. After the fifteen letters have been completed, each player looks at their letters and with the help of a dictionary, begins to create as many different words as possible. The first player or team of players to create a list of fifteen words says, "Dictionary Deadline" and the game ends.

Players check for accuracy of spelling and if all fifteen words are spelled correctly that player earns 15 points.

Here are some doozer definitions:

PARADISE: Two little white cubes with black dots.

HUMDINGER: A person who hums while ringing the bell.

APPEASE: A single serving of green peas!

Spelling

FUN

With

All Kinds

of Words

RACE TO RHYME

PLAYERS:	2 - 4
LEVEL:	Grade 2 and up
SKILLS:	Spelling and identifying rhyming words
EQUIPMENT:	One thirty-sided alphabet die, paper and pencil
GETTING STARTED:	Each player needs their own paper and pencil to record the letters rolled. The goal of the game is to be the first player to make at least two rhyming words. Player one rolls the die and both players record this letter on their paper. Players alternate rolling the die and recording the letters onto their paper. Repeat letters are also recorded. If a ☆ is rolled the roller may choose a letter of their choice which is also recorded by both players.
	When one player notices a combination of letters that spell at least two words that rhyme they say "Rhymers". The player must correctly spell the two words in order to earn a point. Play continues for a set period of time. If players say "Rhymers" at the same time then both players must secretly record their rhyming pair. Players share their words. If the pairs are different and spelled correctly both players earn 1 point each. If the pairs are the same neither player earns a point and play continues. Players continue to build rhyming words and earn a point for each new pair of "rhymers". The player with the most points at the end of the game is the winner.
EXAMPLE:	Letters rolled include: b, f, r, c, j and a. Player one says "rhymers" and verbalizes "bar and far" and spells them outloud. Player earns 1 point and a new round of play begins.
VARIATION:	Extra points can be earned for any additional rhyming words that are found.
	bar/far car/jar. The original pair = 1 point and additional words earn 1 point each.

WORD SHAPES

PLAYERS:	2
LEVEL:	Grade 1 - 3
SKILLS:	Spelling by using word configuration
EQUIPMENT:	One thirty-sided alphabet die, one gameboard per player (see reproducibles)
GETTING STARTED:	The goal of the game is to be the first player to fill in their gameboard with correctly spelled words. Players need to know and recognize the following terms:

Upstairs letter

Main floor letters

Basement letters

Players alternate rolling the die and calling the letters outloud. Both players may choose to use any letter and place it into any space in their gameboard. Players may reject ten rolls along the way. The rejected rolls are recorded in the appropriate spaces on the gameboard. If a player rolls a ☆ players may select any letter of their choice. Once a letter is recorded in any space it cannot be changed or erased. Players must only record appropriate letters into the appropriate shaped spaces.

Both players need to continue to roll until all their spaces are filled in. The player with the most correctly spelled words is the winner.

VARIATION: Play a "Speed Up" variation of word shapes. Players alternate rolling and filling in their shapes until one player has created five correctly spelled words and verbalizes "Word Shapes". This player earns 5 points for that round.

 TEACHING TIP:

Having the shape drawn around the word can help some children visualize the word and connect it to the appropriate letters.

Student Example:

Ricki

8 words ⟩ Score
10 rejects

Strategy

first you need to think of
words that these
shapes, because then it
gives me a better variitie
of words to choose from

WORD SHAPES

1. two

2. at

3. fog

4. then

5. cat

6. had

7. yes

8. we e

9. w nt

10. wag

REJECTS

G	W	Y	M	L
X	V	F	O	Z

55

LETTER LADDERS

PLAYERS: 2

LEVEL: Grade 3 and up

SKILLS: Learning suffixes

EQUIPMENT: One thirty-sided alphabet die, one gameboard per player (see reproducibles), pencil

GETTING STARTED: The goal of the game is to be the player with the most correctly spelled words.

Players alternate rolling the die and calling the letters outloud. Both players may choose to use any letter and place it into any space in their gameboard. Players may reject ten rolls along the way. The rejected rolls are recorded in the appropriate spaces on the gameboard. If a player rolls a ☆ players may select any letter of their choice and record it anywhere on their gameboard. Once a letter is recorded into any space it cannot be changed or erased.

EXAMPLE:

q	u	i	c	k	l	y		7 points
	s	l	o	w	l	y		6 points
		c	u	r	l	y		5 points
			o	n	l	y		4 points
				f	l	y		3 points

Total 25 points

REJECTS

VARIATION: See Reproducibles for other ladders! Also try prefixes <u>re</u>, <u>un</u>, <u>co</u>, <u>de</u>, <u>sub</u>

 TEACHING TIP:

Building word families ie., words ending in "ly" helps establish an understanding of common letter combinations. Teaching by using groups of words that share a spelling pattern helps students make connections.

COMPOUND SNAP

PLAYERS:	2
LEVEL:	Grade 2 and up
SKILLS:	Recognizing compound words
EQUIPMENT:	One thirty-sided alphabet die
GETTING STARTED:	The goal of the game is to be the first player to name a compound word beginning with the letter indicated on the die. Players alternate rolling the die and identifying the letter. If a ☆ is rolled, the die is re-rolled. Players now race to be the first player to give a correct compound word starting with that letter.
EXAMPLE:	ROLL = K
	Acceptable answers include:
	kingfisher, keychain, and keepsake
	Players earn 2 points for saying a correct compound word before their opponent.
	Players continue to alternate rolling the die. After a set period of time the player with the most points is the winner.
VARIATION I:	Players may use an alphabetical gameboard to list and/or record their responses during the game ie.,

airplane	bedroom
courtyard	dogsled
evergreen	firehose

The first player to fill ten compound words in alphabetical sequence is the winner.

VARIATION II: Play a non-competitive variation. Allow players to spell as many compound words as possible during the alotted time. The team who correctly spells the most compound words wins.

 TEACHING TIP:

Compound words are made up of at least two words. Each word must have its own vowel.

ANTSY ANTONYMS

PLAYERS: 2 or teams of 2 vs. 2

LEVEL: Grade 3 and up

SKILLS: Identifying and spelling antonyms

EQUIPMENT: One thirty-sided alphabet die, paper and pencil

GETTING STARTED: The goal of the game is for players to correctly give an antonym pair that is different than their opponents. Players roll the die and identify the starting letter. If a ☆ is rolled the die is re-rolled. Both players now secretly spell an antonym pair using the appropriate letter.

EXAMPLE: Roll = W

Player one secretly records "Wide - Narrow"

Player two secretly records "White - Black"

Once completed, players share their answers. If their antonym pairs are different and spelled correctly players earn 2 points each. If the players words are incorrectly spelled no points are earned. If players have recorded the same antonym pairs both players earn 1 point each.

Play continues for a set number of rounds. The player with the most points is the winner.

VARIATION: Antonym Snap - Players roll the die and identify the starting letter. The first player to correctly give an antonym pair scores a point. Bonus points can be earned for spelling the pair correctly. If a player is incorrect their opponent may have an opportunity to verbalize and spell an antonym pair for 1 point.

Q: What do you get when you cross a family reunion with a picnic?

A: "Ants & Uncles"!

SIMPLY SYNONYMS

PLAYERS: 2 or teams of 2 vs. 2

LEVEL: Grade 3 and up

SKILLS   Identifying and spelling synonyms

EQUIPMENT: One thirty-sided alphabet die, paper and pencil

GETTING STARTED: The goal of the game is for players to give a word and an acceptable synonym for that word with each roll of the die. Player one starts by rolling the die and identifying the starting letter. If a ☆ is rolled, the die is re-rolled. The player may choose any word beginning with this letter, but it must be a word that would have synonyms. Player two must verbalize a synonym for player one's word in order to earn a point. If players are playing in teams, player one must verbalize a word to their partner and the partner must give a correct response for a point.

EXAMPLE: Player one rolls R and chooses the word "rare" and player two gives the synonym "unusual". (Older students may want to check their words using a thesaurus). If the player is correct they earn 1 point. Bonus points may be awarded if the player can provide more than one synonym. ie., "rare, unique, etc.

Player two now takes their turn rolling the die. Play continues for a set period of time. The player with the most points is the winner.

Q: What worm can never go into space?

A: An earthworm.

SYNONYM SNAPPERS

PLAYERS: 3

LEVEL: Grade 3 and up

SKILLS: Identifying synonyms

EQUIPMENT: One thirty-sided alphabet die, thesaurus (optional)

GETTING STARTED: One player is selected to be the roller. This player rolls the die, identifies the starting letter and calls out a word that would have synonyms starting with this letter. If a ☆ is rolled, the die is re-rolled. The other two players now race to be the first player to give an acceptable synonym as their response.

EXAMPLE: Roll = P and roller gives the word: PLAN

Players two and three now must think of an appropriate synonym. Player three says "design" and earns 1 point. Players may check for accuracy in a thesaurus. If both players correctly respond at the same time, both players may earn a point. Play continues until all players have been the roller for an equal amount of turns. The player with the most points is the winner.

 TEACHING TIP:

Teach children to listen for syllables and try to represent each one - don't forget a vowel in each syllable!

TEACHER: What kind of insects are good in school?

CHRIS: Spelling Bees.

60

THINKING THESAURUS

PLAYERS: Teams of 2 vs. 2

LEVEL: Grade 3 and up

SKILLS: Spelling and identifying synonyms

EQUIPMENT: One gameboard per team, regular die, thesaurus, pencil

GETTING STARTED: The goal of the game is for teams to correctly spell an acceptable synonym, with the correct number of syllables before the other team. Both teams have an identical gameboard. Gameboards can be created by the teacher or students to ensure that an appropriate challenge level is created. Some ideas for words may come from thematic units of study in all subject areas.

SAMPLE GAMEBOARD

SYNONYM	WORD
1.	small
2.	big
3.	intelligent
4.	fast
5.	afraid
6.	fierce
7.	unusual
8.	simple
9.	nice
10.	correct

To begin play for the first round a player rolls the die. This number indicates how many syllables the synonym for line number one (ie., in this example small) must be. Players use the following legend to determine number of syllables.

1 or 2 rolled	=	1 syllable word ie., wee
3 or 4 rolled	=	2 syllable word ie., tiny, petite
5 or 6 rolled	=	3 syllable word ie., miniscule

As soon as the die is rolled both teams try to be the first team to correctly spell an acceptable synonym. Once a team has recorded their answer they say "Thinking Thesaurus". They must spell their word correctly and also verify that the word is an acceptable synonym. A thesaurus can be used for this purpose. If a team is correct they may fill in their answer on the appropriate line of their gameboard and both teams proceed to the next line. For each new line the die is re-rolled to determine the number of syllables. After all ten lines are finished players count up the number of filled in words on their gameboards. The team with the most is the winner.

VARIATION: Try similies:

As cold as a _____.

As hot as a _____.

As tall as a _____.

As smart as _____.

As quick as _____.

As poor as _____.

Q: What kind of bug does a cowboy ride?

A: A horsefly.

JOHN: I'm sorry but I can't lend you a dollar.

JANE: Boy, are you cheap.

JOHN: No, I'm not. I just don't believe in passing the buck.

(Jane's Dad will love this one!)

HOMONYM RIDDLES

PLAYERS: 2 or teams of 2 vs. 2

SKILL: Identifying and spelling homonyms

LEVEL: Grade 3 and up

EQUIPMENT: One thirty-sided alphabet die, paper and pencil

GETTING STARTED: The goal of the game is for players to correctly guess and spell a homonym pair. Player one rolls the die and identifies the letter. Player one now uses this letter as the starting letter for the homonym pair riddle that they will give to player two.

EXAMPLE: Player one rolls a P and chooses the homonym "PAIR/PEAR". Player one gives the following riddle to player two: "Two of something". Player two must now figure out the riddle and spell PAIR/PEAR. If the player is able to answer and correctly spell the homonym they earn 1 point. If a ☆ is rolled the player may select any letter of their choice.

Players reverse rolls for the next round. After a set period of time the player with the most points wins.

TEACHING TIP:

When playing in teams have both players on Team A work on one homonym pair together.

Q: What do you get when you cross a mountaintop with a ghost?

A: A peak-a-boo.

GO DIRECTLY TO JAIL

PLAYERS:	Teams of 2 vs. 2
LEVEL:	Grade 3 and up
SKILLS:	Identifying and spelling words that break phonic rules, generalizations
EQUIPMENT:	One thirty-sided alphabet die, one gameboard per team (see reproducibles), pencil
GETTING STARTED:	The goal of the game is to be the first team to fill in all spaces of their gameboard.
	Team one starts by rolling the die and identifying the letter. This letter must be used somewhere in the jail word spelled by the team. Team one must use this letter and spell a word that contains any letter that breaks a spelling/phonic generalization.
	Some examples: the was once eight
EXAMPLE:	Team one rolls T and spells "eight".
	Team one must also explain which letter is breaking a phonic rule.

TEACHING TIP:

Have students collect jail words and post them on a large chart. They can refer to these when spelling. We also had our students place a jail (eight) around any jail word in their writing.

SAMPLE JAIL WORDS

above	eye	iguana	ocean	sure
anybody	eight	issue	orange	tongue
brother	front	love	pigeon	very
come	goes	mother	said	were
does	high	nothing	school	you
doughnut				

Q: What woman fenced in the jail's house?

A: Barb Wire.

GHOST LETTER LINGO

PLAYERS:	Teams of 2 vs. 2
LEVEL:	Grade 3 and up
SKILLS:	Identifying and spelling words with silent letters
EQUIPMENT:	One thirty-sided alphabet die, gameboard (see reproducibles), pencil
GETTING STARTED:	The goal of the game is to be the first team to fill in all spaces of their gameboard. Team one starts by rolling the die and identifying the starting letter. If a ☆ is rolled, the die is re-rolled. This letter must be used somewhere in the ghost word created by the team. Team one must use this letter and spell a word that contains any silent letter.
EXAMPLE:	Roll = B
	The team records "CRUMBS" and records it on the first line of their gameboard. Team two now takes their turn. If a team rolls a letter and they are unable to spell a silent letter word containing that letter, they miss a turn. The other team then proceeds. The first team to fill in all ten spaces on their gameboard is the winner.
VARIATION:	COMPETITIVE PLAY: Teams may alternate rolling the letter to be used in the ghost word. The first team to correctly verbalize a word containing this ghost letter earns 1 point. For an additional point the team may correctly spell their word. The die is re-rolled for the next round.

 TEACHING TIP:

Have children deliberately mispronounce the word to remember odd combinations or silent letters ie., an island "is" land - hard "k" sound "cuh"nee We also put a ghost around silent words in our writing. 😊 knee

---

SAMPLE GHOST WORDS

answer	climb	knew	light	whole
bough	enough	knife	listen	wrapped
bought	high	knock	rough	wrist
catch	honest	know	talk	write
caught	knee	laughed	walk	wrong

Puzzlers, Brainstormers and Word Games

PICTURE BOOK PUZZLES

PLAYERS: 2 or teams of 2 vs. 2

LEVEL: Grade 2 and up

SKILLS: Spelling simple words, initial letter recognition

EQUIPMENT: One thirty-sided alphabet die, alphabet picture book, paper and pencil

GETTING STARTED: The die is rolled to establish which letter (page) of the alphabet book the players must refer to. If a ☆ is rolled, players re-roll the die. Players flip to the corresponding page. The first player to correctly spell any item on the page scores a point. The die is rolled again and players flip to the next corresponding page of the alphabet book. Play continues for a set period of time. The player with the most points is the winner.

VARIATION I. The die is rolled and players or teams turn to the appropriate page. A time limit such as ten minutes is established and players spell as many items on the page as possible. The team with the most words correctly spelled is the winner.

VARIATION II: Play as **variation I** but players also roll two regular dice to determine the length of the words ie., players roll 5 + 2 and players must hunt for seven letter words on the appropriate page to verbalize and spell.

 TEACHING TIP:

There are literally thousands of alphabet picture books available for children. For this game try to pick a picture book with beautiful, rich illustrations so that the spelling and vocabulary development opportunities are maximized. Our favourites are included in the bibliography.

LETTER ROLL

PLAYERS: Solitaire - 2

LEVEL: Grade 2 and up

SKILLS: Creating words with a minimum of two letters

EQUIPMENT: One thirty-sided alphabet die, paper and pencil

GETTING STARTED: The goal of the game is to create as many words as possible using letters which have been placed into a "LETTER BANK", To begin, players build their letter bank by rolling the die twenty times and recording each roll. If the same letter is rolled a second time, it must be recorded again. After the twenty rolls have been completed, each player looks at the letters and begins to create as many different words as possible. Each single letter may only be used once per word unless it appears twice in the letter bank ie., "glass" - s must have been rolled twice.

LETTER BANK

```
K R S A M J

P L O S H G T

T V D E C A B
```

If a ☆ is rolled a player may choose any letter to record in their letter bank.

Player one builds some of the following words: place, lace, please, lost, jog, glass, starve, cab, cost.

After a set period of time each player counts up the number of words created. The player with the most words wins.

VARIATION I: Players count up the letters in each word. A four letter word earns 4 points, a five letter words earns 5 points, etc.

VARIATION II: Players earn BONUS POINTS for rhyming words ie., double points would be earned for **cost** and **lost**.

VARIATION III: Players earn 10 additional BONUS POINTS for creating meaningful sentences. Each new sentence must contain at least four different words from those previously created.

EXAMPLE:

```
X U Y E P D A

F K S V C H

T J Z H I E I
```

1. the	10. jive
2. ship	11. sheet
3. fade	12. sheep
4. sex	13. The six sheep eat chives.
5. six	14. fat
6. fix	15. sat
7. hive	16. hat
8. key	17. sky
9. five	18. The sky is hazy.

 TEACHING TIP:

This game may be introduced as a whole class activity where the teacher records the twenty rolls and prints the letters on chart paper or the chalkboard. During free time or teacher directed time students may work cooperatively in teams or individually to create their words. This activity may continue for several days and scores are accumulated and determined at the end of the week.

WORD BLAST

PLAYERS: 2 - 4

LEVEL: Grade 3 and up

SKILLS: Spelling simple and complex words

EQUIPMENT: One thirty-sided alphabet die, one gameboard per player (see reproducibles), pencil

GETTING STARTED: The goal of the game is to be the first player to use all the letters on their grid by spelling new words.

To begin players alternate rolling the alphabet die and building identical gameboards ie., the first letter rolled is a B and all players record this letter in the first square in the top row of their grid. If after twenty rolls a vowel has not been rolled players agree on one single vowel that can be recorded as well. Once the boards have been filled in with letters, the players sit back to back and say "Blast Off". The spelling portion of the game begins as players try to use all the letters in their grid while creating a list of words. A player cannot use the same letter twice in a word unless it appears in the gameboard twice. Letters can be used in more than one word. All of the letters must be used at least once in order to win. When a player crosses off their last letter used to create a word, they say "Word Blast" and the game ends.

EXAMPLE:

B	S	A	R	F
G	W	X	D	N
C	E	J	O	T
U	Y	R	H	Z

A winning list of words could include:

oxen	gaze	frown	cow
joy	burst	had	

VARIATION: In addition to using every letter in the gameboard, to win the round a player must also construct a sentence using some or all of the words created in their list.

BRAINSTORMERS

PLAYERS:	2 or teams of 2 vs. 2
LEVEL:	Grade 3 and up
SKILLS:	Brainstorming, spelling simple words
EQUIPMENT:	One thirty-sided alphabet die, gameboard (see reproducibles), pencil
GETTING STARTED:	Player or team one rolls the die to determine the brainstorming category for the round. The die is rolled a second time to determine the starting letter for a word that fits the category. If a ☆ is rolled, the die is re-rolled.

CATEGORIES

A = ANIMALS
B = BLUE OR BIG THINGS
C = COUNTRIES OR CITIES
D = DINOSAURS OR DOGS
E = ENVIRONMENT
F = FAIRY TALE WORDS OR FOOD
G = GARDEN OR GARAGE THINGS
H = HOME - THINGS FOUND IN THE
I = INSECTS OR ICKY THINGS
J = THINGS THAT JUMP, JIGGLE OR JINGLE
K = THINGS FOUND IN KITCHENS
L = LOUD OR LIGHT THINGS
M = MUSICAL THINGS
N = NIGHT TIME THINGS
O = ORANGE THINGS
P = PEOPLE'S NAMES
Q = QUICK OR QUIET THINGS
R = ROUND THINGS
S = SCHOOL OR SPORT THINGS
T = TALL OR TINY THINGS
U = UNDER THE SEA
V = VEGETABLES OR VEHICLES
W = WHITE OR WOODEN THINGS
X = ANY WORD WITH AN X IN IT
Y = YELLOW THINGS
Z = THINGS FOUND IN A ZOO

EXAMPLE:

Roll One = B blue or big things

Roll Two = M

Team One spells "monsters" because monsters are big and they begin with M.

If correctly spelled, it is recorded into one of the spaces on the gameboard. Players score 1 point per letter. Monsters = 8 points. If a player cannot think of a word they take a blank space and do not score any points.

BRAINSTORMERS

DAFFODIL (Yellow Things)	**TYRANNOSAURUS** (Dinosaurs)	**JAPAN** (Country)
KIWI (Round Things)	**QUILL** (Light Things)	**TOMATO** (Food)
BANJO (Musical Things)	**NOON HOUR** (School Things)	**LIQUID** (Environment)
PANDA (Animals)	**TIGER** (Zoo)	**AIR** (Night)

VARIATION I:

To decrease the difficulty have players verbalize instead of spell a word that falls into the category beginning with a specific letter.

VARIATION II:

Team Competitive Play - The first team to find a word can spell it and place it into their gameboard. If it is not spelled correctly the opposing team may try. The first team to fill in all spaces with correctly spelled words is the winner.

Q: What do you get when you cross a parrot with an elephant?

A: A bird that uses big words.

74

KEEP IT GOING

PLAYERS: Teams of 2 vs. 2

LEVEL: Grade 3 and up

SKILLS: Brainstorming, spelling simple and/or complex words

EQUIPMENT: One thirty-sided alphabet die, paper and pencil

GETTING STARTED: Players refer to the Categories Reproducible p. 125 and roll the alphabet die to select the category for that round. If a ☆ is rolled, the die is re-rolled. The goal of the game is to verbalize twenty-six words beginning with the letters of the alphabet in sequence that fit into the selected category.

Team one rolls an F and names the category "fairy tale" and /or "food". Players on team one alternate verbalizing words that fit either category beginning with the letter A through Z.

EXAMPLE:

PLAYER ONE	PLAYER TWO
apple	banana
cantaloupe	doughnut
eggplant	fairies
goblins	ham
STOP	

If a player hesitates for ten or more seconds their play is over and they earn 1 point for each correct answer. In the above example team one would earn 8 points .

While team one is verbalizing their answers team two may also earn points by correctly spelling any or all of the words on team one's list. They score 2 points for each correctly spelled word.

Team two begins their turn by rolling a letter to select a new category ie , ROLL = S and players name the category "school" or "supermarket". Play continues for a set period of time or until one team earns 75 points.

EXAMPLE:

ROLL = S "school or supermarket"

PLAYER ONE	PLAYER TWO
adding	books
cashier	desk
encyclopedia	fruit
gym	history
ice cream	juice
ketchup	library
math	noon hour
office	produce
quiet	recess
science	timestable
uniform	vegetables
washroom	exercise
yard	ziplock bags

 TEACHING TIP:

As the teams verbalize the words they may also want to keep in mind some game strategy. For instance, they may choose to verbalize "encyclopedia" rather than eggs because encyclopedia is much more difficult to spell and lessens the opportunity for the "spelling opposition" team to earn 2 points.

An extra player may be appointed as the timer to assist both teams. The timer would be responsible for monitoring the response time and accuracy of the given words.

PARTNERS IN SPELLING

PLAYERS:	2 teams of 2 vs. 2
LEVEL:	Grade 3 and up
SKILLS:	Spelling simple words, problem solving
EQUIPMENT:	Two thirty-sided alphabet die, paper (one "master sheet" for both teams to record on) and pencil
GETTING STARTED:	The goal of the game is to be the last letter placed down to spell a word.

Each player rolls their own five letters and secretly records these on paper. They also select a vowel of their choice for a total of six letters. Players on the same team may look at each others letters but can not talk between themselves.

One player from each team rolls the die and the team with the letter closest to A can choose to start or not to begin the play of the game.

The players on the two teams alternate play throughout the game.

EXAMPLE:

TEAM A
Player one and player two

versus

TEAM B
Player one and player two

TEAM A
Player one's rolls =   C F O N R   A
Player two's rolls =   S H W K E   I

TEAM B
Player one's rolls =   B G I L M   O
Player two's rolls =   U C N P V   A

Team A begins with player one recording an "R" on the master sheet and player two recording a "W". Team B follows with player one recording an "I" and player two recording an "N". Player two now spells the word "win" and Team B earns 3 points for spelling a three letter word. These three letters are circled on the Master Sheet and may not be used again. Team B now offers Team A the choice to lead or not to lead with the next letter.

77

Letter "R" remains on the sheet for the teams to use as it was not previously used to spell "WIN".

ie., R Ⓦ Ⓘ Ⓝ These letters cannot be used again.

Team A chooses to lead and player two records a "K" and player one records a "C".

Team B follows the play with player two recording a "U" and player one recording letter "L". Player one spells "LUCK" and circles letters Ⓛ Ⓤ Ⓒ Ⓚ on the Master Sheet as these letters are now eliminated and cannot be used again. Team B earns 4 points for correctly spelling "LUCK" and once again letter "R" remains on the Master Sheet as it was not used. Team B now asks Team A whether they would like to lead with their next two letters. Team A chooses not to lead.

Player two on Team B now leads with letter "P" and records this on the Master Sheet. Player one records an M. Player one on Team A records an "O" and player two records an "S" and spells "ROMPS". Team A circles these letters on the Master Sheet and earns 5 points for this word.

Team B chooses not to lead and player one on Team A begins with letter "F". Player two follows with letter "H" and both letters are recorded. Player one on Team B records a "B" and player two follows with letter "V".

Player two on Team A records their final letter, "E" and player one records their final letter "N". Player two spells "HEN" and circles these letters on the Master Sheet. Team A earns 3 points for correctly spelling "HEN".

When there are no more vowels left the game ends and both teams add up their accumulative points. The team with the highest score wins.

PUZZLE SPELL

PLAYERS: Solitaire - 2 or teams of 2 vs. 2

LEVEL: Grade 3 and up

SKILLS: Spelling and creating words

EQUIPMENT: One thirty-sided alphabet die, one gameboard per player (see reproducibles), calculator, paper and pencil

GETTING STARTED: Each player needs their own gameboard.

Player one rolls and places the letter rolled in any one square. A player may not erase the letter after it has been recorded. If a ☆ is rolled a player may choose any letter of their choice to record in their puzzle. Players alternate rolling the die placing their letters into their gameboard.

Each player is allowed five reject rolls. If a player rolls any letter and chooses not to use this letter, it is recorded as a reject roll. That player would have four reject rolls left. The player then re-rolls a new letter.

Each player is also allowed five double roll spaces. If a player rolls a letter they would like to record in two different spaces they may do so ie., rolls an S and records this in two different spaces. That player has four double chances left.

When a player has filled in all their puzzle spaces with letters the rolling for that player is over. Players now hunt for correctly spelled words in their puzzle. Each letter of the correctly spelled word is equal to the face value of the square. The player with the most points is the winner.

Student Example:

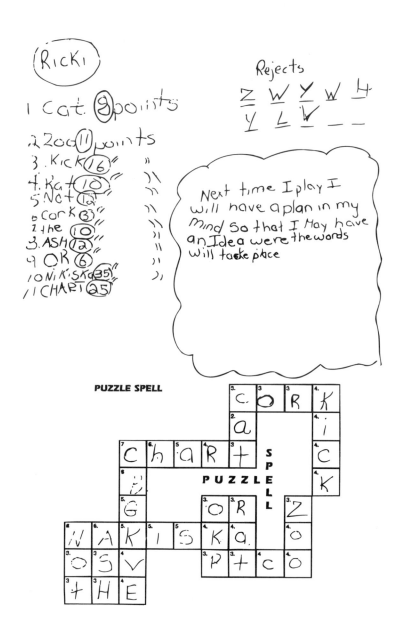

E.T. PHONE HOME

PLAYERS: 2 - 4

LEVEL: Grade 3 and up

SKILLS: Spelling simple words, problem solving using logical reasoning

EQUIPMENT: One thirty-sided alphabet die, paper and pencil

GETTING STARTED: The goal of the game is to be the first player to complete at least five telephone number endings. Each player has their own gameboard. Gameboards can be created by the teacher or students to ensure an appropriate challenge level is created. Players alternate rolling the die and calling the letters outloud. Both players may choose to use any letter and place it into any space in their gameboard. Once a letter is recorded in any space it cannot be changed or erased. Players may choose not to use a letter when it is called but can not go back and use it at a later time.

Once a player has filled in five meaningful telephone endings they say "E.T. Phone Home", and share their answers. If they are accepted by the other players, then they are the winner for that round.

EXAMPLE: LAST 4 DIGITS

1. ___ ___ ___ ___   shoe store

2. ___ ___ ___ ___   florists shop

3. ___ ___ ___ ___   veterinarian

4. ___ ___ ___ ___   hospital

5. ___ ___ ___ ___   gas station

6. ___ ___ ___ ___   coffee shop

7. ___ ___ ___ ___   school

8. ___ ___ ___ ___   barber shop

Acceptable answers may include in order:
1. feet, shoe or sole
2. bulb, rose or fern
3. pets or help
4. sick or well
etc.

VARIATION: Have students figure out the telephone number combination using the following code found on a typical telephone:

a b c 1	d e f 2	g h i 3
j k l 4	m n o 5	p q r 6
s t u 7	v w x 8	y z 9

ie., feet = 2227

 TEACHING TIP:

Have students decide the telephone number clues before playing. They can record these beside the 4-digit blank before they start playing. See reproducibles.

CHAMELEONS

PLAYERS:	2 or solitaire
LEVEL:	Grade 3 and up
SKILLS:	Spelling simple words, problem solving
EQUIPMENT:	One thirty-sided alphabet die, paper and pencil
GETTING STARTED:	Each player verbalizes a four letter word of their choice and records it on their paper. The goal of the game is to be the first player to change their word to a new word with the resulting final word including no more than one letter in its original position ie., "lake": to "lend or robe", etc. Players alternate rolling the die.

Players are allowed to reject any roll. A maximum of fifteen rolls per round may be taken by both players. Nonsense words are unavoidable and often necessary during the process of changing a word. If a ☆ is rolled players may select any letter of their choice.

PLAYER ONE SOCK	PLAYER TWO NEST

1. Roll = B
   Bock
	1. Roll = N
	   Nent

2. Roll = Q
   reject
	2. Roll = K
	   nenk

3. Roll = U
   Buck
	3. Roll = S
	   senk

4. Roll = WILD
   Bucs
	4. Roll = T
	   reject

5. Roll = I
   reject
	5. Roll = J
	   reject

6. Roll = H
   rejects
	6. Roll = I
	   SINK

Player two is the first player to create a new four letter word and earns 1 point for that round. Players select new four letter words to begin the next round of play.

VARIATION:	Players may choose to create longer words. The goal of the game is to be the first player to change their word with the final word including no more than two letters in their original positions.

DON'T BREAK THE CHAIN

PLAYERS:	2
LEVEL:	Grade 4 and up
SKILLS:	Beginning and ending letters, spelling
EQUIPMENT:	One thirty-sided alphabet die, paper and pencil
GETTING STARTED:	The goal of the game is for players to keep the chain of words going. The first player to break the chain loses the round. To begin the die is rolled to determine the first letter of the first word for the round. ie., Roll = E. Player one must then roll the die a second time to determine which letter this E word must end with. Player one rolls a G and spells EGG. Player two must now keep the chain going. The last letter of the previously spelled word becomes the first letter of the next word - in this example G. Player two rolls the die to determine what their word must end in. Player two rolls an R and spells the word GULPER. Player one must now spell a word starting with R and must roll to determine the ending letter. If a ☆ is rolled the player may select any letter of their choice.

Play continues until one player is not able to spell a word with the given beginning and ending letters. The player who breaks the chain loses that round and the other player scores 1 point. The player with the most points after a set period of time is the winner.

 TEACHING TIP:

Have both players record all answers to practise spelling their words and to create a visual "chain" of words. ie.

Player 1	Player 2	Player 1	Player 2	Player 1	Player 2	Player 1
EGG	GULPER	ROAM	MOM	MICA	AX	Strikes Out

VARIATION: Play cooperatively with teams working together to keep the chain going. The team that creates the longest word chain would win that round.

"SPACEY" SPELLING

PLAYERS:	Solitaire or 2
LEVEL:	Grade 3 and up
SKILLS:	Word recognition, spelling simple words
EQUIPMENT:	One thirty-sided alphabet die, one gameboard per player (see reproducibles), pencil
GETTING STARTED:	The goal of the game is to spell the most words using the letters in your gameboard. Words must be created using the letters in horizontal, vertical or diagonal sequence. Both forward and backward directions are acceptable (see example). Each player needs their own gameboard. To begin players record any two vowels into any two spaces of their choice. Players now roll to fill in each row of their gameboards starting in the first square of the top row and ending in the last square of the bottom row. If a ☆ is rolled the player may choose any letter to fill in the square.

Once the grid has been completely filled in the players may begin to look for any correctly spelled words with a minimum of two letters. The players circle the words and spell them in list form in the space provided on their gameboard.

The player with the most correctly spelled words wins.

EXAMPLE:

T	R	D	B	O	X
C	L	I	N	F	E
K	P	K	J	O	P
Q	S	K	R	N	Z
L	O	L	I	P	O

OR
BOX
IN
NO   NO   NO
SO
OF   OF
LIP
ON   ON   ON
KID

85

Student Example:

Ricki

Score: 38 points

It is better to place your letters so you can make words within words.

H	N	Z	D	i	P
O	H	B	O	X	B
T	R	Y	h	O	u
W	h	Oo	O	h	S
i	G	E	W	u	i
N	Z	L	B	O	X

hi/hi	Six	u s/us
Box	Win	Twin
the	Be	ox/ox
TRY	Bus/Bus	Hot
in	OH	Or
Who	Row	OW
Hog	go	Sub/sub
BY	how	you
Box	who	Zoo
Zoos	DO	DID
Leo	Boo	we

GRID LOCKED

PLAYERS:	2 or teams of 2 vs. 2
LEVEL:	Grade 3 and up
SKILLS:	Spelling simple/complex words
EQUIPMENT:	One thirty-sided alphabet die, one gameboard per player or team (see reproducibles), pencil
GETTING STARTED:	The goal of the game is for players to make as many two, three, four, five, and six letter words as possible. Players alternate rolling the die and saying the letter outloud. Both players place this letter anywhere in their grid but once it is placed it cannot be changed or erased. If a player rolls a ☆ both players may choose any letter of their choice.
	Players continue rolling the die until the gameboards are complete. After the rolls are completed players figure out how many two, three, four, five, and six letter words have been correctly spelled in their grid either horizontally, vertically or diagonally.
SCORING:	Players score 2 points for a two-letter word, 3 points for a three-letter word, etc.
	The player with the most points is the winner.

EXAMPLE:

D	E	R	A	S	E
N	Z	K	H	T	L
A	T	Q	J	A	O
M	X	K	J	L	M
E	P	S	O	B	W
W	Q	U	N	E	W

ON	MAN	NAME	ERASE
BE	MEW	MOLE	BLAST
AN	RED	LAST	
AT	HAM		
HA	SOB		
AX	RED		
NO	ARE		
UP	NEW		
16 points	24 points	12 points	10 points

87

TEACHING TIP:

It may be easier for players to list the words correctly spelled in their gameboard as they are created. Players may wish to circle them on the grid during the play of the game.

TEACHING TIP:

As players place their letters have them keep in mind the strategy of looking for small words that make up a larger one ie., "star" is composed of "star", "tar" and backwards "rat", and "rats"!

TEACHER: Spell "little".

MADISON: L-i-t-t-t-l-e.

TEACHER: Leave out one of the t's.

MADISON: Which one?

TEACHER: Mackenzie, why is it so difficult for you to learn how to spell?

MACKENZIE: Because you keep changing the words.

CLUE ME IN

PLAYERS: 4, 2 teams of 2 vs. 2

LEVEL: Grade 4 and up

SKILLS: Spelling simple words, giving definitions

EQUIPMENT: One thirty-sided alphabet die, paper and pencil

GETTING STARTED: The goal of the game is to be the team to solve and spell their mystery words in the fewest clues possible.

STEP ONE: To begin each player rolls their own bank of ten letters which all players can see throughout the game. Each player then spells one mystery word using some or all of their letters. This mystery word is kept hidden from their partner and their opponents.

STEP TWO: After the mystery word has been chosen each player must create a list of six single word clues that will help their own partner guess the mystery word in STEP THREE.

EXAMPLE:

TEAM ONE	TEAM TWO
STEP ONE:	
Player One:	Player One:
J S H R O E N C D P	X N W B A L S H M I
Player Two:	Player Two:
T E G K M O Q U I	R E Y S G A N R O Z

STEP TWO: SECRET WORD

Player One:	Player One:
PHONE	SNAIL
Player Two:	Player Two:
QUIT	ORANGE

Player One's Clue List For PHONE		Player One's Clue List For SNAIL	
Points 6.	call	Points 6.	bug
5.	talk	5.	slimy
4.	distance	4.	slow
3.	quarter	3.	water
2.	ring	2.	shell
1.	busy	1.	eat

89

STEP THREE:

Both teams roll to determine which team goes first. The team closest to A begins. Players attempt to guess each others mystery words in the least amount of clues. ie., Player one on Team One begins by giving their first clue CALL. If their partner guesses and spells PHONE on the first clue 6 points are earned. Player one continues to offer clues to their partner until there are no clues left (no points are earned) or until a correct guess is made. The team earns points according to how many clues were given. Team Two now takes their turn. After all four players have given their clues the game ends. The team with the most points wins.

VARIATION: Visual Memory Challenge - Players may only see the letters for one minute before STEP TWO and STEP THREE begin.

 TEACHING TIP:

One Mnemonic strategy is to construct a simple sentence using the letters of a word (also an old trick from studying bones in anatomy) ie., to remember how to spell <u>because</u> - <u>b</u>aby <u>e</u>lephants <u>c</u>an <u>a</u>ll <u>u</u>se <u>s</u>mall <u>e</u>ars. Have students construct their <u>own</u> sentences to help them remember their "tough" words.

Sentence Construction and Parts of Speech

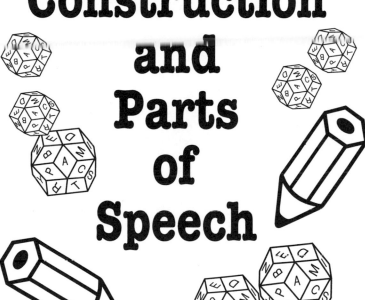

ROLL A SENTENCE

PLAYERS: 2

LEVEL: Grade 2 and up

SKILLS: Constructing simple sentences

EQUIPMENT: One thirty-sided alphabet die, paper and pencil

GETTING STARTED: The goal of the game is to be the first player to construct and verbalize a meaningful, grammatically correct sentence, using the letters rolled as the starting letters for each word. (see example)

Players alternate rolling the die and calling the letters outloud. If a player rolls a ☆ they may choose a letter of their choice.

Players should record the letters as they are rolled. Once a player is able to construct a sentence they say "Roll a Sentence" and verbalize their sentence. If they are correct they earn 5 points. The first player to score 50 points is the winner.

EXAMPLE: Letters rolled in sequence included: X B C D F and T

Player two uses B,C,D,F,T and verbalizes:

"The boy caught five dragonflies."

5 points are scored.

CONNOR: Everynight I take two quarters to bed with me.

MACKENZIE: Why?

CONNOR: They're my sleeping quarters.

I WANT TO BE SENTENCED

PLAYERS: 2 or teams of 2 vs. 2

LEVEL: Grade 2 and up

SKILLS: Constructing simple sentences

EQUIPMENT: One thirty-sided alphabet die, paper and pencil

GETTING STARTED: The goal of the game is to construct a simple sentence using the first letters generated by the roll of the die in sequence. Player one rolls for player two. Player one rolls a B. Player two begins to build a sentence beginning with any "B" word of their choice. Player one continues to roll for player two until that player has constructed a simple sentence. Players earn 1 point for each word correctly spelled in their sentence. Maximum ten words per sentence.

EXAMPLE: Player One Rolls: B,M,P,W,F,H and L

Player two constructed the following sentence: "Before Monday Peter will finish his laundry."

Player two earns 7 points.

Player two now begins rolling for player number one. If a ☆ is rolled the "constructing" player may select any letter of their choice.

Play continues for a set period of time. When both teams have had the same number of turns, the game ends. The player with the most points is the winner.

VARIATION: To decrease the level of difficulty the player may change any word in their sentence at any time but the words must remain in sequence to the letters rolled.

Q: What happens to words when they break the law?

A: They get sentenced.

R U LONG WINDED?

PLAYERS: 2

LEVEL: Grade 2 and up

SKILLS: Constructing simple sentences

EQUIPMENT: Paper and pencil, two regular dice

GETTING STARTED: The goal of the game is for players to successfully construct sentences using the required number of words. Players use the following legend to determine the length of sentence they must make:

GRADE 1 - 2: Roll one die
1 = re-roll
2 = re-roll
3 = 3 word sentence
4 = 4 word sentence
5 = 5 word sentence
6 = 6 word sentence

GRADE 3 and up: Roll two dice and add the roll.
2 = re-roll
3 = 3 word sentence
4 = 4 word sentence
5 = 5 word sentence
6 = 6 word sentence
7 = 7 word sentence
ETC.

Player one rolls the dice to establish the length of the sentence player two must construct. If the player responds correctly they earn 1 point per word. Players can also record their sentences and try to incorporate accurate spelling. Player two now rolls the dice for player one, who must now construct their sentence.

Players continue to alternate turns rolling the dice. The first player to score 50 points is the winner.

ALLITERATION ACROBATS

PLAYERS: 2

LEVEL: Grade 3 and up

SKILLS: Creating alliterative sentences

EQUIPMENT: One thirty-sided alphabet die, one regular die, paper and pencil

GETTING STARTED: The goal of the game is to create an alliterative sentence. Player one rolls both dice and must construct an alliterative sentence using the following legend:

Roll 1 or 2 roll again
Roll 3 create a three word sentence
Roll 4 create a four word sentence
Roll 5 create a five word sentence
Roll 6 create a six word sentence

Each word must start with the letter indicated on the alphabet die. If a ☆ is rolled, the die is re-rolled. Linking words are not allowed. ie., the, with, on, etc.

EXAMPLE: Roll 5 and M

Madison mixed Mackenzie's marvellous meal.

Roll 6 and B

Baby bears bite big black bugs.

Players score 1 point for each word in their sentence. Play continues for a set period of time. The player with the most points is the winner or play to 50 points.

VARIATION: To decrease the level of difficulty, players are allowed one or two linking words for sentences containing more than 4 words.

Q: What kind of language do ticks speak?

A: Tick talk.

ALPHABETICAL HOP

PLAYERS :	2
LEVEL:	Grade 3 and up
SKILLS:	Spelling words, constructing meaningful sentences
EQUIPMENT:	Two regular dice, one alphabet line per player (see reproducibles), paper and pencil
GETTING STARTED:	The goal of the game is to be the first player to correctly construct and spell a meaningful sentence. Each player starts the game on letter M on their alphabet board. Player one rolls the dice and chooses to add, subtract, multiply or divide the numbers to generate the number of "alphabetical hops" they may take either forward or backward on their alphabet line.
EXAMPLE:	Roll 5 and 1
	Player one can either add: 5 + 1 = 6 or subtract: 5 - 1 = 4 or multiply: 5 x 1 = 5 or divide: 5 ÷ 1 = 5. Player one selects one of the numbers and may move either forward or backwards from letter M on their alphabet line. The letter the player falls on is used as the starting letter of the first word of the players' sentence.
	Player one chooses 5 + 1 = 6 and moves ahead six spaces to letter S, M n o p q r S
	Player creates the first word of their sentence: "Sometimes"
	Players alternate turns.
	Player one rolls 5 and 2 on their second turn and can do the following : 5 + 2 = 7, 5 - 2 = 3 or 5 x 2 = 10. Player one chooses 5 - 2 = 3 and moves three spaces backwards to letter P and continues their sentence: "Sometimes people..."
	Players continue to alternate turns rolling the die and moving to a new letter for the next word. The first player to construct and spell a meaningful sentence wins the round.
EXAMPLE:	Player one's sentence at the end of the game was:
	SOMETIMES PEOPLE WILL QUIT.

Player one's third roll was 5 + 2 = 7. Seven hops from P = W. Players one's fourth roll was 3 X 2 = 6. Six hops back from W = Q.

Roll 3 was 5 and 2. 5 + 2 = 7. Seven hops from P = W.

Other acceptables sentences would be:

Seven penguins walked quickly.

Some pupils wrote quizzes.

etc.

Q: What did the mother grasshopper say to her children?

A: Hop to it.

PREPOSITIONS PLEASE

PLAYERS: 2 - 4

LEVEL: Grade 2 and up

SKILLS: Identifying prepositions, constructing sentences, using prepositions

EQUIPMENT: One regular six-sided die, one reproducible gameboard, colored markers, or bingo chips

GETTING STARTED: The goal of the game is to be the first player to cover five spaces in any direction on their "preposition" gameboard.

Each player rolls their die once. The player with the highest roll goes first. Each player has a preposition 'WHERE" card. Players alternate rolling the die and covering the appropriate space and preposition on their gameboard.

W ⚀	H ⚁	E ⚂	R ⚃	E ⚄
on	above	before	to	in
against	with	over	from	beside
next to	off	across	between	after
by	out	behind	below	under

If a player rolls a ⚀ that player may choose to cover any one preposition word under the "W" on their board. If a player rolls a ⚁, any one preposition word under the letter "H" may be covered, etc. If a player rolls a ⚂, this is considered a WILD ROLL and the player may cover any one space of their choice on their gameboard. Before placing a bingo chip on their "preposition" space, the player must use that preposition in a sentence and verbalize this outloud to the other players. To increase the difficulty, players may also record their sentence on paper.

99

EXAMPLE:	"OFF" The cup fell OFF the table.
	"BESIDE" The house is BESIDE the river.
	The first player to get five in a row horizontally, or four in a row vertically or diagonally wins that round.
VARIATION:	Players can agree that only a horizontal row is acceptable or just vertical or diagonal.

TEACHING TIP:

A preposition is a word that shows relationship of position, direction, or time between the words in a sentence ie., with, for, at, and, in, are.

TEACHER:	Did your father help you with these word puzzle problems?
CONNOR:	No, teacher. I got them wrong all by myself.

SNAPPY SENTENCE FILLERS

PLAYERS: 2 equal skill level

LEVEL: Grade 3 and up

SKILLS: Constructing meaningful sentences, identifying parts of speech

EQUIPMENT: One thirty-sided alphabet die, one gameboard per player (teacher or student generated), pencil

GETTING STARTED: The goal of the game is to be the first player to fill in all spaces of their gameboard with correctly spelled words. Gameboards can be created by the teacher or students themselves to ensure that an appropriate challenge level is created. Some ideas for sentence fillers may be based upon thematic units of study in all subject areas. Both players must have an identical gameboard for play.

Play begins by rolling the die and identifying the letter. This letter may be used as the starting letter for any word that would fit in any open space on the gameboard. The first player to say "Fillers" and spell an appropriate word may fill it in. The die is rolled again and players again try to spell an appropriate word for any of the other available spaces. The first player to complete their gameboard is the winner.

EXAMPLE: 1. She fell off the _____.
                           (noun)

                        2. The teachers asked the children to _____.
                           (verb)

                        3. Saturday is a great day for _____.
                           (verb)

                        4. We ate _____ for dinner.
                           (noun)

                        5. The store is having a _____ sale on _____.
                           (adjective)   (noun)

                        6. At the beach we saw _____ _____.
                           (adjective)   (noun)

                        etc.

PARTS OF SPEECH PIZZAZ

PLAYERS: 2 or teams of 2 vs. 2

LEVEL: Grade 4 and up

SKILLS: Identifying parts of speech, spelling

EQUIPMENT: One thirty-sided alphabet die, one regular die, one gameboard per player (see reproducibles), paper and pencil

GETTING STARTED: Players use the following legend for the regular die roll:

1 = noun
2 = verb
3 = adjective
4 = adverb
5 = preposition / interjection
6 = players choose any part of speech

The goal of the game is to be the first player to fill in all spaces of their gameboard with correctly spelled words. Player one rolls the alphabet die and identifies the starting letter for their word. If a ☆ is rolled the player may choose the letter of their choice. The regular die is rolled to indicate the type of word the player must spell. ie., Roll = M and 3.

Player one must spell an adjective beginning with the letter M. Some possible words might include: mauve, merry, mischievious, etc.

Player one must correctly spell their chosen word before filling it into the appropriate space on their gameboard. If they cannot spell it, or cannot think of an appropriate word, then nothing is filled in. Player two now takes their turn. Players continue to alternate turns. The first player to fill in their gameboard is the winner.

 TEACHING TIP:

An interjection is a word that shows an exclamation of surprise, sorrow, delight or some other emotion ie., Oh! Ah! Hurray!

SPEEDY PARTS OF SPEECH

PLAYERS: 2 or teams of 2 vs. 2

LEVELS: Grade 4 and up

SKILLS: Identifying parts of speech: verbs, nouns, adjectives, spelling words

EQUIPMENT: One thirty-sided alphabet die, gameboard (see reproducibles), pencil

GETTING STARTED: Each player needs their own gameboard. The goal of the game is to be the first player to fill in all spaces of their gameboard with correctly spelled words. Player one rolls the die. Both players now race to verbalize either a verb, noun, or adjective starting with the letter. Player one rolls an R and player two verbalizes "ran - verb". Player two must now correctly spell that word before filling it into the appropriate space on their gameboard. If the word is spelled correctly it is recorded and a new letter is rolled. If the player does not spell the word correctly, then their opponent has the opportunity to verbalize and spell a word starting with the letter rolled. If successful, they fill this word into their gameboard and a new letter is rolled for the next round. If a ☆ is rolled, players re-roll the die.

Players continue to alternate rolling the die. The first player to complete their gameboard is the winner.

EXAMPLE:

VERBS	NOUNS	ADJECTIVES
RAN	BOAT	YELLOW
KICKED	OLIVE	TIGHT
FLEW	JET	SHINY
CALL	MOUSE	DARK

VARIATION: Non-competitive play. Players play cooperatively as teams and work together to fill in all spaces of their gameboard after only one roll of the die ie., an S is rolled and players must fill in all spaces of their gameboard with words beginning with the letter S.

Roll = S

VERBS	NOUNS	ADJECTIVES
SLID	SOFA	SILKY
SKIPPED	SCHOOL	SLIMY
SNORED	SANDWICH	SUNNY
SKATED	SNAKE	STINKY

Teams work together to complete their gameboard. Teams check each other's boards for accuracy and earn 1 point for each correctly spelled response.

 TEACHING TIP:

Knowing the Etymology (history of words) can help with spelling. Origin is indicated in the dictionary entry. By collecting words and putting them into word origin categories students can make some spelling generalizations. ie., rodeo, mosquito, pueblo.

ROLL EM ... AND ACTION

PLAYERS: 2

LEVEL: Grade 4 and up

SKILLS: Identifying verbs, spelling

EQUIPMENT: One thirty-sided alphabet die, gameboard (see repro-ducibles), paper and pencil

GETTING STARTED: Each player needs their own gameboard. The goal of the game is to be the first player to fill in all spaces on their gameboard with correctly spelled verbs. Player one rolls the die. If a ☆ is rolled, the die is re-rolled. Both players now race to spell a verb starting with that letter.

When a player has spelled a word, that player calls "action" and spells their word to their opponent. If the word is a verb and is spelled correctly, it is recorded into the player's gameboard and a new letter is rolled.

If the player does not spell the word correctly, then their opponent has the opportunity to spell a word starting with the letter rolled. If successful, they fill this word into their gameboard and a new letter is rolled for the next round.

Players continue alternating rolling the die. The first player to complete their gameboard is the winner.

VARIATION: Try nouns, adjectives or adverbs.

TEACHER: Name two pronouns.

CHRIS: Who, me?

TEACHER: That's correct!

Oh No! Not Another Cliche!

PLAYERS: Teams of 2 vs. 2

LEVEL: Grade 4 and up

SKILLS: Minimal cue, spelling simple/complex words

EQUIPMENT: Student constructed gameboard (for ideas see reproducibles), paper and pencil

GETTING STARTED: The goal of the game is to be the first team to solve their "Hidden Cliches". To begin both teams secretly select five cliches from the reproducible list. Both teams now decide which letters to remove from their five cliches before they are exchanged for the second part of the game.

EXAMPLE: Team one's cliches with letters removed for team two to solve:

1. __s t__ __ ck a__ __hi_v__s.

2. T__e m__r__ __h__ __e__ri__r.

3. E__ __y __o__e __as__ __o.

4. B__ __t__r __a__e t__a__ __ev__r.

5. A __i__e a __o__en.

(Teams may create more than five.)

As a guide line:

- Four or five word cliches minimum seven letters removed.

- Three word cliches minimum five letters removed.

The level of students will determine changes to the above guidelines.

Once both teams have completed their "Hidden Cliches" the lists are exchanged. Team one now selects any five letters. If any of these letters appear in the Hidden Cliche they are filled in by Team two. Team two also selects five letters and they are filled in by team one. Players now have time (3 - 5 minutes) to solve their cliches. At the end of the time limit teams share their answers. Teams earn 5 points per correctly spelled cliche. The team with the most points is the winner.

Here is a list of the percent frequencies of the letters of the alphabet in ordinary English.

E	13
T	9
A,O	8
N	7
I,R	6.5
S,H,D	6
L	3.5
C,U,M	3
F,P,Y	2
W,G,B	1.5
V	1
K,X,J	0.5
Q,Z	0.2

DISAPPEARING ALPHABET
FROM A TO ZEE
HOW DOES IT SOUND?
ALPHABETICAL HOP

| a b c d e f g h i j k l m n o p q r s t u v w x y z |
| A B C D E F G H I J K L M N O P Q R S T U V W X Y Z |
| a b c d e f g h i j k l m n o p q r s t u v w x y z |
| A B C D E F G H I J K L M N O P Q R S T U V W X Y Z |

ABC BINGO

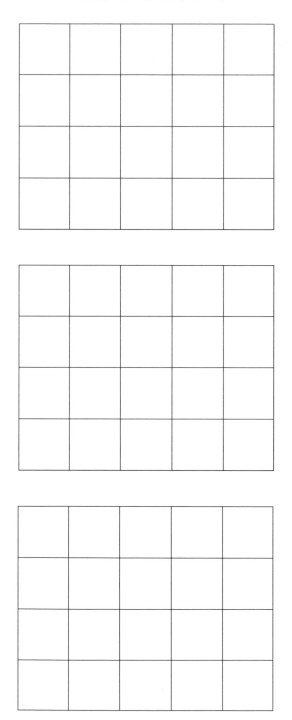

BINGO BLASTERS

A	B	☆	C	D	E
☆	F	G	H	I	☆
J	K	L	M	N	O
P	☆	Q	R	S	T
U	V	W	X	Y	Z

A	B	☆	C	D	E
☆	F	G	H	I	☆
J	K	L	M	N	O
P	☆	Q	R	S	T
U	V	W	X	Y	Z

WORD RACE

BEGINNERS

_____AT	_____ACK	_____AN	_____AD
_____EG	_____EN	_____ET	___ELL
_____IN	_____IP	___ICK	_____ID
___OCK	_____OG	_____OT	___OP
___UB	_____UN	___UNK	___UG

DOUBLE MIDDLES

__TT ___	__NN __	___NN __	___MM __
__DD ___	__DD __	___DD __	___DD __

WHAT'S IN THE MIDDLE?

B_____T   S_____T   R____G   D_____G

BEGINNERS

GA_____	HA _____	MA_____	TA _____
GE_____	HE _____	ME_____	TE_____
GI _____	HI _____	MI _____	TI _____
GO ____	HO _____	MO ____	TO_____
GU_____	HU _____	MU ____	TU_____

REJECT ROLLS

_____   _____   _____   _____

VOWEL CROSSES

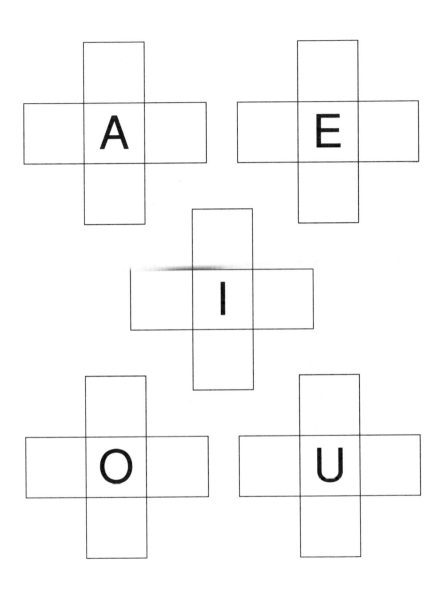

REJECT ROLLS

VOWEL CROSSES

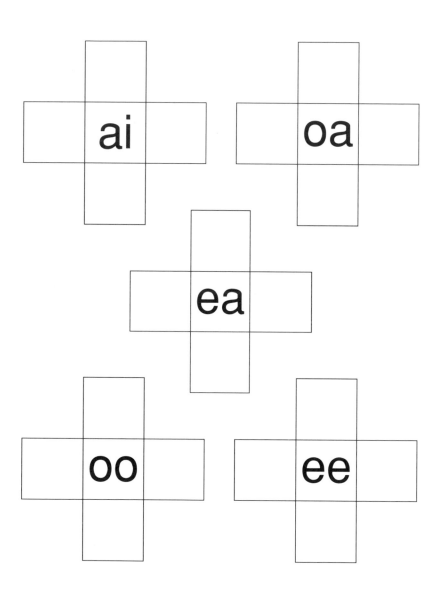

REJECT ROLLS

UP TO YOUR NECK IN WORDS

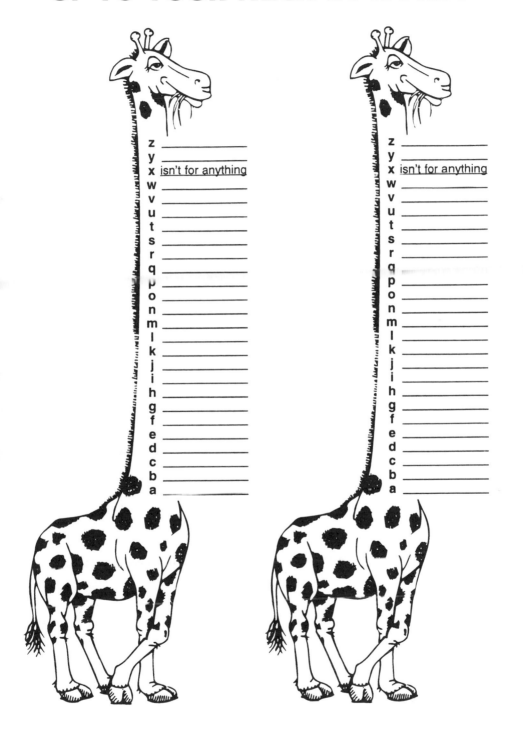

z _____
y _____
x isn't for anything
w _____
v _____
u _____
t _____
s _____
r _____
q _____
p _____
o _____
n _____
m _____
l _____
k _____
j _____
i _____
h _____
g _____
f _____
e _____
d _____
c _____
b _____
a _____

z _____
y _____
x isn't for anything
w _____
v _____
u _____
t _____
s _____
r _____
q _____
p _____
o _____
n _____
m _____
l _____
k _____
j _____
i _____
h _____
g _____
f _____
e _____
d _____
c _____
b _____
a _____

ALPHABET ROLL-OUT

A B C D E F G H I J K L M
N O P Q R S T U V W X Y Z

Player One	Player Two
_____ _____	_____ _____
_____ _____	_____ _____
_____ _____	_____ _____
_____ _____	_____ _____
_____ _____	_____ _____
_____	_____

2 letter words	3 letter words	4 letter words
_____	_____	_____
_____	_____	_____
_____	_____	_____
_____	_____	_____
_____	_____	_____
_____	_____	_____
_____	_____	_____
_____	_____	_____
_____	_____	_____
_____	_____	
_____		

WORD SHAPES

1.

2.

3.

4.

5.

6.

7.

8.

9.

10.

REJECTS

LETTER LADDERS

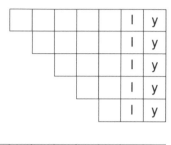

						l	y	7 points
						l	y	6 points
						l	y	5 points
						l	y	4 points
						l	y	3 points

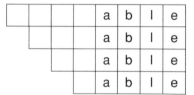

					n	e	s	s	9 points
					n	e	s	s	8 points	ness = "state of"
					n	e	s	s	7 points
					n	e	s	s	6 points

			a	b	l	e	8 points
			a	b	l	e	7 points	able = "can do"
			a	b	l	e	6 points
			a	b	l	e	5 points

			m	e	n	t	10 points
			m	e	n	t	9 points	ment = "state of"
			m	e	n	t	8 points
			m	e	n	t	7 points

Other Letter Ladders to Try…

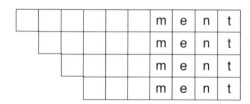

t i o n   f u l   l e s s   e s t   e r

o u s   i z e   n e s s

i n g   i e d   e d

Plurals

s   e s   i e s

120

GO DIRECTLY TO JAIL

JAIL

1. _____   4. _____   7. _____

2. _____   5. _____   8. _____

3. _____   6. _____   9. _____

JAIL

1. _____   4. _____   7. _____

2. _____   5. _____   8. _____

3. _____   6. _____   9. _____

JAIL

1. _____   4. _____   7. _____

2. _____   5. _____   8. _____

3. _____   6. _____   9. _____

GHOST LETTER LINGO

Ghost
Letter
Lingo

1. _____   6. _____

2. _____   7. _____

3. _____   8. _____

4. _____   9. _____

5. _____   10. _____

WORD BLAST

BRAINSTORMERS

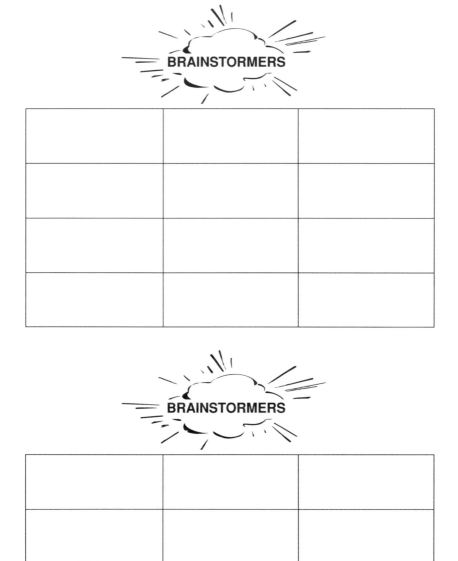

CATEGORIES REPRODUCIBLE

A = ANIMALS

B = BLUE OR BIG THINGS

C = COUNTRIES OR CITIES

D = DINOSAURS OR DOGS

E = ENVIRONMENT

F = FAIRY TALE WORDS OR FOOD

G = GARDEN OR GARAGE THINGS

H = HOME - THINGS FOUND IN THE

I = INSECTS OR ICKY THINGS

J = THINGS THAT JUMP, JIGGLE OR JINGLE

K = THINGS FOUND IN KITCHENS

L = LOUD OR LIGHT THINGS

M = MUSICAL THINGS

N = NIGHT TIME THINGS

0 = ORANGE THINGS

P = PEOPLE'S NAMES

Q = QUICK OR QUIET THINGS

R = ROUND THINGS

S = SCHOOL OR SPORT THINGS

T = TALL OR TINY THINGS

U = UNDER THE SEA

V = VEGETABLES OR VEHICLES

W = WHITE OR WOODEN THINGS

X = ANY WORD WITH AN X IN IT

Y = YELLOW THINGS

Z = THINGS FOUND IN A ZOO

PUZZLE SPELL

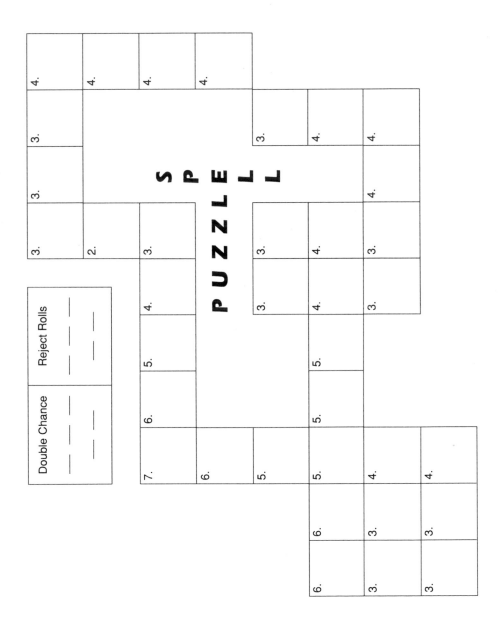

E.T. PHONE HOME

LAST 4 DIGITS	CLUE
1. ____ ____ ____ ____	
2. ____ ____ ____ ____	
3. ____ ____ ____ ____	
4. ____ ____ ____ ____	
5. ____ ____ ____ ____	
6. ____ ____ ____ ____	
7. ____ ____ ____ ____	
8. ____ ____ ____ ____	
9. ____ ____ ____ ____	
10. ____ ____ ____ ____	

LAST 4 DIGITS	CLUE
1. ____ ____ ____ ____	
2. ____ ____ ____ ____	
3. ____ ____ ____ ____	
4. ____ ____ ____ ____	
5. ____ ____ ____ ____	
6. ____ ____ ____ ____	
7. ____ ____ ____ ____	
8. ____ ____ ____ ____	
9. ____ ____ ____ ____	
10. ____ ____ ____ ____	

SOME POSSIBLE CLUES:

hairdresser, church, fitness club, movie theatre, bakery, sporting goods store, optometrist, gas station, dry cleaners, printer, school, bookstore, car dealership.

"SPACEY"SPELLING

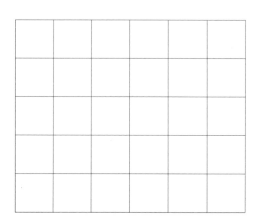

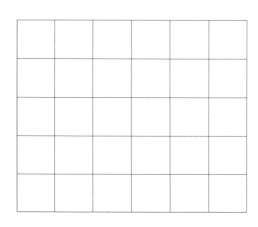

GRID LOCKED

2 letter words	3 letter words	4 letter words	5 letter words	6 letter words
_____	_____	_____	_____	_____
_____	_____	_____	_____	_____
_____	_____	_____	_____	_____
_____	_____	_____	_____	_____
_____	_____	_____	_____	_____
_____	_____	_____	_____	_____
_____	_____	_____	_____	_____
_____	_____	_____	_____	_____
_____	_____	_____	_____	_____
_____	_____	_____	_____	_____

PREPOSITIONS PLEASE

W ⚀	H ⚁	E ⚂	R ⚃	E ⚄
on	above	before	to	in
against	with	over	from	beside
next to	off	across	between	after
by	out	behind	below	under

W ⚀	H ⚁	E ⚂	R ⚃	E ⚄
on	above	before	to	in
against	with	over	from	beside
next to	off	across	between	after
by	out	behind	below	under

PARTS OF SPEECH PIZZAZZ

NOUN	VERB	ADJECTIVE	ADVERB	PREPOSITION

NOUN	VERB	ADJECTIVE	ADVERB	PREPOSITION

NOUN	VERB	ADJECTIVE	ADVERB	PREPOSITION

SPEEDY PARTS OF SPEECH

VERBS	NOUNS	ADJECTIVES

VERBS	NOUNS	ADJECTIVES

VERBS	NOUNS	ADJECTIVES

ROLL EM' AND ACTION

**ROLL EM'
AND ACTION!**

1.	2.	3.
4.	5.	6.
7.	8.	9.
10.	11.	12.

**ROLL EM'
AND ACTION!**

1.	2.	3.
4.	5.	6.
7.	8.	9.
10.	11.	12.

OH NO! NOT ANOTHER CLICHE

1. As quick as a bunny
2. The more the merrier
3. Faster than a speeding bullet
4. As thick as thieves
5. Never in a million years
6. A needle in a haystack
7. Easy come easy go
8. As slow as molasses in January
9. Two heads are better than one
10. Hungry as a horse
11. You win some, you lose some
12. It's the cat's meow
13. A stitch in time
14. Cold as a cucumber
15. It's a small world
16. Living the life of Ryley
17. Whistle while you work
18. Easy does it
19. Birds of a feather
20. It's raining cats and dogs
21. By the grace of God
22. Skinny as a rail
23. Blind as a bat
24. White as a ghost
25. Slim pickings
26. Beggers can't be choosers
27. Crafty as a fox
28. His better half
29. All in a day's work
30. Forever and a day
31. Neat as a pin
32. Good things come in small packages
33. Better luck next time
34. Clean as a whistle
35. Once upon a time
36. Time flies when you're having fun
37. Tough as nails
38. Fit as a fiddle
39. Slept like a log (baby)
40. Dropped it like a hot potato
41. Fight like cats and dogs
42. Shaking like a leaf
43. Works like a dream
44. Warm as toast
45. Cute as a button
46. As fast as lightning
47. Flat as a pancake
48. Naked as a jailbird
49. Tight as a drum
50. Hungry as wolves
51. A chip off the old block
52. The plot thickens
53. Pure and simple
54. Home sweet home
55. Last but not least
56. Where there's a will there's a way
57. Cheeks like roses
58. A fool and his money are soon parted
59. Don't look a gift horse in the mouth
60. The apple doesn't fall far from the tree.

JANE FELLING and JOANNE CURRAH are co-authors of Box Cars and one-Eyed Jacks, volumes I, II, and III. Also winners of a National Learning Disabilities Award, they travel across Canada doing school-based workshops and author visits. They are based in Edmonton, Alberta. Their books cover numeration, all operations, place value, graphing, data gathering, co-operative games, and integers. Their games involve problem solving and can be adapted to suit the needs of all students as well as to complement any existing math program.

Jane was a speaker at the 1994 BCPTA Fall Conference in Vancouver.

The article outlines an author visit to a southern Alberta school and some of the math activities undertaken.

Box Cars and One-Eyed Jacks
Math Games Using Cards and Dice

We have been fortunate to be invited to work in many schools in an "authors in residence" format. During a typical author visit, we teach math games to over 400 students and get to meet and talk with over 30 teachers. The following experience in southern Alberta is typical of teachers who see the benefit of using math games in their mathematics program. They have taken our ideas and implemented them in a way that fits and works for them. In all our workshops, we suggest starting math backpacks and share with participants the following story:

Scene: An elementary school in Alberta

We quickly prepared for our next scheduled class by placing the cards and dice on the tables. Scanning our timetable, we noted a group of 25 Grade 3 students were on their way. As we do with all groups we work with we greeted them at the door with a quick welcome and "find a seat and get ready to play." We weren't prepared for the long line of neon backpacks making their way into our classroom. One eager student explained, "We don't need to use your cards and dice we all have our own – see." The class was in the process of unzipping their packs, taking out their cards and dice when the teacher approached us to explain, "I couldn't resist, I found these packs at a Loonie Store and thought they would be perfect for math backpacks. The kids know that after school they can take their math backpacks home. Instead of math homework, they have math play."

This is but one example of how easy it is to start a math backpack program.

Why math games backpacks?

1. Many primary students are used to taking home At–Home readers or other activities. Why not "add +" some math to the take home backpack for a change.

2. Children are normally eager to play games. Math games are as willingly played by our most frustrated and reluctant math

students as by our math whizzes. Homework became Homeplay.

3. It is a welcome change for parents who often have to struggle with their children to complete homework activities. Parents and children become partners and can learn together in a more relaxed setting. The cards and dice can be a welcome change to paper and pencil practice.

4. Games can be individualised by a teacher to fit a students needs or interests. Games can be used to introduce, practice or review a concept. They are also excellent for students who have to be absent from school for extended periods of time due to illness or vacation.

Getting started

It is best to send a letter home to parents introducing the Math Games Backpack program. Meet the Teacher Night is an opportune time to discuss the purpose of at-home practice with math games. Time permitting, try teaching the parents one game—especially if the children are also in attendance. As well, it will help if the students learn a repertoire of games before the backpacks start going home.

Have available suitable carrying cases—backpacks, laminated envelopes, ziplock bags etc., game instructions and materials (cards, dice, any reproducible gameboards) for the class; one per child is ideal. Once under way, most children can take home a game two or three times a week.

Children make the best teachers

One of the best ways to ensure "backpack success" is to have the students act as teachers at home. Children enjoy teaching the games to their family members; they thrive on being the expert. More important, their understanding of the math concept develops by introducing the games, rules, and mathematical concepts as they repeatedly teach at home. Both familiar and new games are sent home once the program is under way.

Developing a mathematical community

Parents were very supportive of the backpack program. Since our time in the classroom, we have found ample evidence to support having parents practise math through games with their children.

One study researched the benefits of having parents work with their children on mathematics using a games approach (Tregaskis, 1991). Seven-and eight-year-old students identified as being in the bottom third of the class were randomly selected to participate in the project, and a control group was established. The three-month study involved training the parents from the experimental group to work with their children. The importance of active listening and using math language was emphasized. During the study, a new game, introduced weekly, was played daily at home. At the end of the three months, the experimental group was more able to remember their number facts and was able to use a broader range of strategies than the control group.

To strengthen the home link in our classrooms, we included space for parents to comment on the math-game experience. A space was provided on the game instructions. The feedback gave us important information.

- How the parent viewed the child's mathematical development.

- Successes, frustrations, and possible solutions that occurred while playing at home. (This helped us to choose future backpack activities.)

- Insight as to any pressure a child was experiencing. On one occasion, a parent commented that the child hadn't "mastered" the facts yet—the child had just started Grade 1. This feedback provided an opportunity to discuss curriculum expectations with the parent earlier than the scheduled interviews.

As these samples show, comments were usually very positive and helpful and served to motivate us to continue the Math Games Backpack Program.

To get you rolling...

Included with the samples are two games that will get you off to a good backpackstart. The games require only a simple deck of cards or dice. In no time at all, you'll be "dealing" with parental and student requests for more games. Enjoy!

Sample letter to parents

Dear Grade 1 parents,

This year, your child's math program will include a games component. Key concepts will be repeated and practised through games in class and at home with the Math Games Backpacks.

Math backpacks will come home for the night, approximately two times a week, with your child. All materials should be returned the next day so that other children in the class can have their turn.

Included in the backpack are the rules for the math game, equipment, and a games book. The games book is for the students and parents to write about their experiences with the game—what they learned, liked about the game, tips to pass on to other classmates, etc. The children will need help with this for the first part of the year. Please help write down their messages for them.

Practice times do not need to be long; 10 to 15 minutes a day will "add up" over the course of the year and will benefit your child's mathematical development greatly.

Math games can be played with brothers or sisters as well. New games will be put into the backpacks every two weeks or so. If you have any special requests (e.g., games for adding, etc.), let me know.

Look forward to the first games arriving home next week. Please enjoy, and return the game bag the next day. Call if you have any questions.

Thank you.

Comments by parents from "Odd or Even?" game

Good game! He was having a hard time with odds and evens before the card game. I think he knows them much better.

Good game! It really encouraged a lot of decision-making and strategy as well as math skills.

Paul enjoys card games. A great way to spend time together and help to strengthen his math skills.

We also played that you could eliminate the cards with the same value of each die or the total of both.

Odd or Even

Skills   Addition to ten, odd and even

Players   Two or more

Equipment   Each player cards (Ace = 1)—10,
                two dice

Getting   Each player arranges his/her cards as
started   follows:

1   3   5   7   9
2   4   6   8   10

Before players begin, they predict which
set of numbers they will eliminate first:
either the odd or the even set. Players
then take turns rolling one or two dice
and begin eliminating sums of their rolls.

Example   Roll 2 and 4: remove 6
                Roll 5 and 3: remove 8

Players continue to take turns until one
player has removed all his/her cards. He/
she receives 10 points for doing so. If the
player also made a correct prediction
(odd or even set first), he/she earns an
additional 5 points.

Play continues to 50 or 100 points.

Variation   Encourage players to add or subtract
                the dice before removing cards. Have
                players remove up to two cards per
                roll.

Addition War

Skills   Addition

Players   Two

Equipment   Grades 1–2 (ace = 1), 5
                Grades 2–3 (ace = 1), 9

Getting   Players divide cards evenly between
started   themselves. Each player turns over
                two cards and adds them together.
                The higher sum gets all the cards. In
                the event of a tie (each player has the
                same sum), WAR is declared. Each
                player deals out three more cards face
                down and then turns over two more
                cards. These two cards are added
                together. The higher sum wins all
                the cards. Play continues until one
                player has collected all the cards
                dealt.

Example | Player 1 | Player 2 |
                |----------|----------|
                | 2 + 3 = 5 | 4 + 1 = 5 |

                War is declared
                (Three cards face down)

                —   —
                —   —
                —   —

                4 + 3 = 7   6 + 2 = 8

                Player 2 collects all the cards.

Variation   Vary the number of cards to modify the
                level of difficulty.

Example   23   or   534
                +6   +43
                Three cards/player   Five cards/player

GENERAL BIBLIOGRAPHY

BASE, Graeme - ANIMALIA,
Stoddart Publishing, 1987. ISBN 0 7737 2206 8

BISHOP, G. - A APPLE PIE
Oxford University Press, 1987. ISBN 0 10 558164 4

BLADES, Ann - BY THE SEA ALPHABET BOOK
Kids Can Press, 1985. ISBN 0 919964 64 8

BOYNTON, S. - A IS FOR ANGRY
Workman Publishing, 1987. ISBN 0 89480 507 X

BRUCE, L. - AMAZING ALPHABETS
Francis Lincoln Ltd., 1993. ISBN 0 7112 0759 3

BURNINGHAM, John - JOHN BURNIGHAM'S ABC
Crown Publishing, 1985. ISBN 0 517 55960 9

COOP, P. & C. - GOING BUGG
Lerner Publishers, Minneapolis. 1986.

ECKSTEIN, J. & GLEIT, J. - The Best Joke Book for Kids #2
Avon Books, 1987.

EICHENBERG, Fritz - APE IN A CAPE
HBJ, 1980. ISBN 0 15 203722 5

FEELINGS, Muriel - JAMBO MEANS HELLO SWAHILI ALPHABET
BOOK
Pied Piper Books, 1974, 1981. ISBN 0 8037 4428 5.

HARRISON, Ted - THE NORTHERN ALPHABET
Tundra Books, 1982. ISBN 0 88776 1925

NATURE ABC
Key Porter Books, 1989. ISBN 1 55013 143 5

LOBEL, Anita - ON MARKET STREET
Scholastic, 1981. ISBN 0590 37179 7

MAC DONALD, Suse - ALPHABATICS
Bradbury Press, 1986. ISBN 002 761520 0

MARTIN, JR., Bill - CHICKA CHICKA BOOM BOOM
Simon & Schuster, 1989. ISBN 0 671 67949 X

MOAK, A. - A BIG CITY ABC
Tundra Book, 1984. ISBN 088776 161 5

MAYER, Mercer - LITTLE MONSTERS ALPHABET BOOK
Golden Press, 1978. ISBN 0 307 11847 9

KNOWLTON, J. - GEOGRAPHY FROM A TO Z
Ty Crowell, 1988. ISBN 0 690 04616 2

PALLOTTA, J. - THE BIRD ALPHABET BOOK
Charlesbridge, 1986. ISBN 0 881106 451 3 also
THE ICKY BUG ALPHABET BOOK
THE OCEAN ALPHABET BOOK
THE FLOWER ALPHABET BOOK
THE YUCKY REPTILE ALPHABET BOOK

PETERSON, S. - WHAT'S YOUR NAME?
Lerner Publishers, Minneapolis, 1987.

PILCHER, S. - ELFABIT
Hayes, 1982. ISBN 0 88625 042 0

SCHULTZ, S. - 101 SCHOOL JOKES
Lerner Publishers, Minneapolis, 1982.

DR. SEUSS'S ABC
Random House, 1963.

TERBAN, M. - EIGHT ATE   A FEAST OF HOMONYM RIDDLES
Clarion Books, 1982. ISBN 0 89919 067 7

VOGEL, M.G. - THE BIG BOOK OF JOKES AND RIDDLES
Playmore Inc., 1978.

WALTON, R. & A. - CAN YOU MATCH THIS?
Lerner Publishers, Minneapolis, 1986.

WILKS, Mike - THE ULTIMATE ALPHABET
Henry Holt, 1986. ISBN 0 8050 0076 3

ABOUT THE AUTHORS

The BOX CARS & ONE-EYED JACKS team of Joanne Currah and Jane Felling bring both innovation and inspiration to their consulting. They have combined expertise in elementary and special education, and have conducted extensive research into the area of Games as a Teaching Strategy. The authors developed all of the games for Volume I while teaching in their classrooms. Since the original publication in 1989, the authors have been successfully inservicing across Canada and the United States. In 1991 BOX CARS & ONE-EYED JACKS won a National Award from the Learning Disabilities Association. During 1992 BOX CARS & ONE-EYED JACKS Volumes II and III were published to meet the growing demand by teachers and parents for new material. Both Vol I and II went on to receive National Best Seller Status in Canada. Their materials now extend Kindergarten to Grade 9 and incorporate the use of cards, dice, special 10, 12, 20 and 30-sided dice. In 1994, "Money Matters for Kids Volume IV" and "Math Games for Kids Using 30-Sided Dice Volume V", were published. "On a Roll to Spelling", published 1995, leads the authors in a brand new direction with their games. Eagerly awaited by both teachers and parents, "On a Roll to Spelling" is sure to be a favourite.

Their newest ventures lead them to the Orient for the development of special educational cards, and importation of special dice. The authors have expanded their inservice and travel extensively. As well as presenting workshops at professional development days, they now offer an *"Authors in Residence"* format where they visit schools and teach the games to students and teachers in their classrooms. They continue to maintain this vital link with children.

box cars and one-eyed jacks™

PRICE LIST 1995

Make cheques payable to:
Box Cars & One-Eyed Jacks

3930 - 78 Avenue
Edmonton, Alberta, Canada
T6B 2W4
Phone 1-403-440-MATH
Fax 1-403-440-1619
GST R135980407

SEND TO: NAME _____

STREET _____

CITY _____ PROVINCE/STATE _____ CODE _____

TELEPHONE _____ DATE _____

BOOKS			QUANTITY	TOTAL
Box Cars and One-Eyed Jacks Vol I	K-4	$20.00	_____	_____
Box Cars and One-Eyed Jacks Vol. II	1-9	$20.00	_____	_____
Box Cars and One-Eyed Jacks Vol. III (comes with 6 special dice)	1-9	$20.00	_____	_____
Set of Box Cars Volumes I, II, III		$50.00	_____	_____
Box Cars and One-Eyed Jacks Money Matters for Kids, Vol. IV	1-9	$20.00	_____	_____
Box Cars and One-Eyed Jacks 30-Sided Dice Games, Vol. V				
(comes with 4 special dice)	K-9	$24.00	_____	_____
Box Cars and One-Eyed Jacks version française (comes with 6 special dice)		$28.00	_____	_____
On a Roll to Spelling...and More (games using special alphabet dice)	K - 7	$22.00	_____	_____
Stratedice (comes with gamebook, tray and 36 dice)	1 - 9	$12.00	_____	_____
Tray and 36 dice (only)	1 - 9	$ 8.00	_____	_____
3 trays and 108 dice	1 - 9	$20.00	_____	_____
Puzzle Island (spelling-story book)	1 - 6	$12.00	_____	_____

DICE		QUANTITY	TOTAL
Regular Dice	5 / $1.00	_____	_____
Manipulite Dice	$1.00/pair, $10.00/6 pairs, $20.00/25 pairs	_____	_____
10 sided (spotted 0-9)	$1.50 each	_____	_____
10 sided (0-9)	$1.00 each	_____	_____
12 sided (1-12)	$1.00 each	_____	_____
20 sided (1-20)	$1.00 each	_____	_____
30 sided (1-30)	$2.50 each	_____	_____
6 sided (0-5)	$1.00 each	_____	_____
Operation (+ - x ÷)	$1.00 each	_____	_____
Overhead Dice	$7.50 pair	_____	_____
* Alphabet 30-sided dice	$2.50 each	_____	_____
Number Jumbler (grades 3 and up)	$8.00 each	_____	_____
Stellar Speller (grades 3 and up)	$8.00 each	_____	_____

PLAYING CARDS		QUANTITY	TOTAL
Special Decks with 11, 12, and 0 cards	$2.50 each or 5 decks/$10.00	_____	_____
Giant Demonstration Deck - 7" x 4-3/4"	$10.00	_____	_____

OVERHEAD TRANSPARENCIES		QUANTITY	TOTAL
Set of Black & Red Overheads (includes 4 sheets = 84 cards total) Ace-King	$10.00	_____	_____
Set of Black & Red Overheads to Match Special Decks (with 11, 12, 0)			
(includes 4 sheets = 84 cards total)	$10.00	_____	_____
Money Overheads (includes 2 sheets of all coins - 133 total/ grey & copper)	$ 5.00	_____	_____

		QUANTITY	TOTAL
ALPHABET TILES 120 Upper case letters	$10.00	_____	_____
MONEY Canadian Coins - Plastic coins including pennies, nickels, dimes, quarters and loonies (130 coins total)	$ 9.50	_____	_____
BINGO CHIPS Red, Green or Amber (200 / pkg.)	$ 2.00	_____	_____
BOX CARS & ONE-EYED JACKS T-SHIRTS (L, XL)	$ 16.00	_____	_____
BOX CARS BASICS PRIMARY KIT	$ 55.00	_____	_____
BOX CARS BASICS INTERMEDIATE KIT	$ 55.00	_____	_____
SPELLING KIT	$ 87.00	_____	_____
MONEY MATTERS KIT	$ 30.00	_____	_____
DELUXE PRIMARY BOX CARS & ONE-EYED JACKS KIT	$269.50	_____	_____
DELUXE INTERMEDIATE BOX CARS & ONE-EYED JACKS KIT	$269.50	_____	_____

SUBTOTAL _____

SHIPPING & HANDLING (single item $4.00) _____ $6.00

(Prices may vary according to large orders)   G.S.T. _____

(Prices subject to change without notice)   **TOTAL** _____

* Available September, 1995   Please allow 3 - 6 weeks for delivery

The Box Cars Team
is available to conduct
the following workshops:

BOX CARS & ONE-EYED JACKS - VOLUMES I, II, III, V

LEVELS: K-3, 4-6, 7-9, Special Needs, Parents

Participants play a selection of math games that use only cards, dice and special dice from BOX CARS & ONE-EYED JACKS Volume I, II, III & V. The games cover numeration, all operations, place value, graphing, data gathering, cooperative games, and integers. Problem solving is integrated into the games. The games can be adapted to suit the needs of all students and will complement any existing math program. Come prepared to play!

This session can also be conducted in French to complement BOX CARS & ONE-EYED JACKS versions françaises.

BOX CARS & ONE-EYED JACKS - MONEY GAMES FOR KIDS, VOLUME IV

LEVELS: K-4, 5-9

Kids love money and they love games. So it seemed natural to pair the Box Cars Math Game format with the teaching of money concepts. Come prepared to play new card and dice games that teach money concepts, problem solving, probability and the operations. Whole class activities to teach real life connections will also be shared.

PARTICIPANTS NEED TO BRING ASSORTED CHANGE TO THIS SESSION.

Come prepared to play.

AUTHOR IN RESIDENCE/MODEL LESSONS

LEVELS: Elementary - Junior High

The authors visit a school for a day and TEACH as many students as possible. Teachers watch, play and learn strategies right along with their "real students" and see how it works. This format is often combined with a Family Fun Night.

BOX CARS & ONE-EYED JACKS - FAMILY FUN NIGHTS

The authors are pleased to launch this new workshop format for parents and children. Typically done in the early evening, these workshops have proven successful in getting HOME AND SCHOOL working together. Think about Meet the Teacher Nights, Parent Interviews, Education Week, Parent Interaction Days, or Summer Send Off. The authors are flexible with scheduling and developing a timetable that suits the school community. The Box Cars games are taught to both parents and children. Strategies to help children with math concepts are shared with the audience as they play.

HOST AN EVENING IN YOUR AREA.

BOX-CARS & ONE-EYED JACKS - ON A ROLL TO SPELLING AND MORE   LEVELS: K-3, 4-7

Over 50 games for kids ages 5 and up. Includes games and spelling strategies that teach: letter recognition, sound/symbol relationships, initial consonants/vowels, spelling simple/complex words, rhyming words, word shapes, syllables, silent letters, rule breakers, homonyms, synonyms, antonyms, brainstormers, puzzlers, constructing sentences/parts of speech.

COME PREPARED TO PLAY!